'Carl Trueman affirms the h
clarity and with excellent judg
ture, the atonement, justification, the importance of systematic theology, and
of the historic creeds and confessions, are here given a ringing affirmation.
Dr. Trueman is fearful that at the very time when our crazy world needs
the four-square gospel more than ever it is being seriously weakened by the
influence of postmodernism, consumerism, and the loss of a sense of history,
both in the church and the Christian academy. The author would be happy
enough if these essays make you think, but happier still if they persuade you
to think – and to act – as an unashamed evangelical.'

Paul Helm,
Emeritus Professor,
University of London

'Carl Trueman throws open the darkened windows of superficiality which
have closed in on the 21st century Western Evangelical Church in order
to allow the fresh, bracing breeze of robust evangelical thought to do its
revitalising work. Dr. Trueman is not afraid to allow any contemporary
idea or practice pass unchallenged, no matter how hallowed by 'evangelical' consensus. But this is not the cheap point scoring of tabloid theology.
Rather it comprises careful, well thought out analysis and comment, deeply
grounded in biblical and reformed theology which is applied with refreshing
clarity and precision.

Dr. Trueman has the wit of a modern day evangelical Chesterton, the prophetic insight of a Francis Schaeffer and the accessibility of a John Stott. This
is a book to read and re-read. It is a very much needed "tract for our times".'

Melvin Tinker,
St John's Parish Church, Newlands,
Hull, England

'Volumes of collected essays depend not on the topic so much as the author
to draw our interest. I cannot think of a young evangelical writer and theologian whose works I more eagerly read than Carl Trueman.'

Mark Dever,
Capitol Hill Baptist Church,
Washington, D.C.

'Carl Trueman has become well known in recent years as an academic historian, taking hold of the torch from scholars like Richard Muller and carrying it further. His painstaking and rigorous scholarship have been of great benefit to evangelicals working in the Reformation and post-Reformation periods. The first part of the book is of this order. In the second part of the book, however, Trueman breaks free, abandons the courtesies of modern academic debate, and lets rip! Here we have short, sharp and exciting thoughts on everything from Psalm singing to the homosexual debate within the Anglican Church. His brilliant caricatures and hilarious asides do not detract from his careful thought but rather help to demonstrate a wisdom and clarity much needed today. You will be entertained and educated by this book.'

A.T.B. McGowan,
Highland Theological College,
Dingwall, Scotland

'One of Carl Trueman's central assertions in this book is the importance of words. God is a personal, speaking God, and is revealed to us both in the incarnate Word and in the written Word of Scripture. Words are at the heart of Reformation theology and at the heart of all true piety. This collection of essays and observations shows that the author not only recognises these facts, but emulates them: as a master wordsmith himself, his approach to a variety of issues demonstrates his desire and creative ability to apply the whole of the Bible to the whole of life. It will challenge, stimulate, inform and teach. It contains a wealth of wisdom in small compass, and confirms Dr. Trueman's place as one of contemporary evangelicalism's most dynamic young theologians.'

Iain D. Campbell
Back Free Church of Scotland,
Isle of Lewis, Scotland

The Wages of Spin:

Critical Writings on Historic and Contemporary Evangelicalism

Carl R. Trueman

ⅯENTOR

Carl R. Trueman is currently teaching Church History and Historical Theology at Westminster Theological Seminary in Philadelphia, having previously been on faculty at the Universities of Nottingham and Aberdeen. He has published numerous books and articles on Reformed theology in the sixteenth and seventeenth centuries, in addition to editing the theological journal, *Themelios*, for UCCF/IFES. He is married to Catriona, and has two sons, John and Peter.

© Carl R. Trueman

ISBN 1-85792-994-2
ISBN 978-1-85792-994-2

Published in 2004
Reprinted 2007
in the
Mentor Imprint
by
Christian Focus Publications
Geanies House, Fearn, Ross-shire,
IV20 1TW, Scotland, UK.

www.christianfocus.com

edited by Malcolm Maclean
cover design by Alister MacInnes

Printed and Bound by
CPD, Wales

CONTENTS

To

Reverend Iver Martin

Dr Ian R. Macdonald

And
'The Colonel'
Donald Matheson

INTRODUCTION

All of the essays and shorter pieces in this volume are drawn from the work I have done over the last five or six years for various evangelical groups in Great Britain and Europe, and they therefore represent something of an eclectic mix, dealing with issues from television to worship. If they have a unity it is perhaps that provided either by my concern to avoid selling out our evangelical birthright to every wind of cultural criticism or trendy new idea that comes our way – I am convinced that Christianity, as an historical religion, needs to listen very carefully to its history in order to build on past strengths and avoid repetition of past mistakes – or by my desire always to provoke readers not only into thinking for themselves but, above all, into having an opinion about things that matter. Too many today sit on the moral and theological fence; too few have any strong opinions about anything. That is why so often theological and ecclesiastical discussion in evangelical circles goes by default, with nobody having clear enough convictions about anything to engage in real discussion. This is not helped, of course, by the increasing tendency in evangelical circles to ape American linguini-spine culture and to regard disagreement with anyone on anything in our allegedly postmodern world as always inherently oppressive. Some evangelicals, indeed, seem to think that the whole point of having a debate is – well, just to have a debate, a conversation, and then to agree to differ as we all sit around having a mutually affirming, self-congratulatory love-fest. I say that such a view is total rubbish. As the late Frankie Howerd would have said, 'Nay, nay, thrice nay!' The point of a debate, as Paul so clearly demonstrates time and again in the Book of Acts, is to establish which position is best; and yes, I for one am still so hopelessly in thrall to modernism, as my relativist critics will no doubt allege, as to believe that some positions (e.g., sacrificing my children to Molech) are not as good as others (e.g., bringing

them up to love and fear the Lord), no matter where you may
be in the world, and no matter to which culture you happen to
belong. That is why I write the way I do – love what I say, hate
what I say, either are acceptable responses; but please try not to
be indifferent to what I say. Indifference, the plague of modern
Western culture in general and evangelicalism in particular,
is at best the result of intellectual laziness, at worst a sign of
moral abdication.

Of course, my own thinking has changed over the years
– only a fool never alters his mind on anything. I now, I think,
have a much better grasp of the cross-cultural and class issues
involved in the theological enterprise – emigration to the USA,
and conversations with colleagues at Westminster Theological
Seminary such as Manny Ortiz, Jeff Jue, Bill Edgar, Dick Gaffin,
Stafford Carson, Susan Post and Scott Oliphint have all served
to give me a better appreciation of both the Reformed tradition
and its place in the modern world than I had when I wrote most
of these pieces. Yet, for all of the lacunae I now see as I reread
them, I still basically stand by what these pieces essentially say;
and I still think a combination of plain speaking, occasional
over-statement, and black humour is the best way to provoke
people to think for themselves. It has always served me well in
the classroom; I hope it does so here.

Many of these essays started life as talks for student groups or
pieces for *Themelios*, the theological student journal I have edited
for UCCF since 1998. I hope they are intellectually stimulating
but I do not present any of them as polished pieces of scholarship; they are rather introductory salvoes and journalistic jabs
at some of the issues which are most pressing for the British
evangelical scene at the moment. The depth of bibliography and
footnoting varies; and those looking for more in-depth discussion of many of the issues raised, particularly in Part One, should
chase up the references which I give for further discussion of
the matters in hand but not assume that my notes give them an
exhaustive scholarly apparatus. These are addresses for students
wanting some stimulation and some guidance at the very start

of their lives as Christians and theologians, and that has shaped the way they are written.

Many Christians and friends have helped me think about these issues over the years – too many to mention here; but I should mention my wife Catriona and my two boys, John and Peter, none of whom may ever read a word of what I write, but whose patience with my not infrequent absences from home on theological business has made the whole possible; Martin Kenunu, close friend and fine scholar, who graciously commented on an earlier draft; Simon Gathercole, Daniel Strange and the other Young Turks at *Themelios* with whom I have so enjoyed working over the years, and who know the importance of having fun and not taking oneself – or anyone else, for that matter – too seriously when it comes to theology; Bob Horn and Ranald MacAulay who have both been sources of encouragement and sound wisdom; and also – perhaps especially – Elizabeth Fraser, whose patience with all of us involved with RTSF is remarkable, whose diligent work for *Themelios* is so invaluable, and whose constant prayers for the whole team have been such a tremendous blessing.

Finally, the book is dedicated to Rev. Iver Martin, my former minister in Aberdeen, now minister of the Free Church of Scotland in Stornoway, Dr. Ian R. Macdonald, the Aberdeen session clerk, known to all affectionately as 'Dr. Ian', and Mr. Donald Matheson, 'the Colonel,' elder in the Free Church of Scotland and mentor to generations of Aberdeen Free Church students. These are men whose humility, learning, friendship and robust Christian testimony has meant more both to me and to my wife, Catriona, over the years than I can express. This book is offered as a small token of my esteem, affection, and gratitude.

Carl R. Trueman
January 2004

PART ONE

EVANGELICAL ESSAYS

ONE

RECKONING WITH THE PAST
IN AN ANTI-HISTORICAL AGE

As I prepared this article I was reminded of the very first issue of the English journal, *The Evangelical Quarterly*, which was issued in January 1929 as part of a concerted attempt to articulate the historic Christian faith in times that were not particularly well suited to such an endeavour. On the back cover of that issue is a series of names of those who had agreed to write articles for the journal. Among the names are those of Professors Ridderbos and Schilder of Kampen. The presence of their names on that list speaks volumes about the consistent ecumenical desire of Reformed theologians throughout the ages to propagate their faith in an intelligent and articulate manner; about their desire to combat heresy while at the same time engaging in well-mannered dialogue with those with whom they disagree.[1] It would indeed have been very opportune for this article if the programmatic statement about the Reformed faith which that journal's first issue contained had been written by a Dutchman – and from my personal perspective, had I been editor I would certainly have arranged it thus – but, as a matter of fact, that honour was accorded to an American, Caspar Wistar Hodge. In an essay of twenty pages or so, Hodge expounded the basic principles of the Reformed faith in a context which showed both his knowledge of its historic origins and emphases and the looming crises which it faced. Indeed, his remarks on the ris-

---

This chapter was originally given as a lecture at the Theological University of Kampen to the Gereformeerde Kerken (Vrijgemaakt) in June 2001.

1. The term 'Reformed' is used throughout this article to refer to the tradition of theology which attempts to place itself self-consciously in the tradition of thought epitomised by the ancient creeds of the church and the confessions and catechisms of the Reformation.

ing Swiss star, Karl Barth, offer us insights into early orthodox responses to the new theology. More than that, they remind us that 1929 was a transition point in the history of Reformed theology, a time when great change was about to sweep over the Reformed world. In the closing paragraph, Hodge makes the following comment:

> Doubtless this Reformed Faith is suffering a decline in the theological world today. What has been termed 'Reformed spring-time in Germany' we cannot regard as the legitimate daughter of the classic Reformed Faith. In Scotland the names of William Cunningham and Thomas Crawford no longer exert the influence we wish they did. In America the influence of Charles Hodge, Robert Breckinridge, James Thornwell, Robert Dabney, William G.T. Shedd, and Benjamin Warfield, seems largely to have vanished.

This list reads almost as a metaphorical obituary for Reformed theology, being as it is a litany of dead Reformed theologians, with Warfield – the most recently deceased – having been dead at that point for eight years. If Hodge had had a less Anglo-American focus he might also have added the names of Kuyper and Bavinck, who died in 1920 and 1921 respectively. The times they were indeed a-changing and, in retrospect, we can see that 1929, witnessing as it did the reorganisation of Princeton Theological Seminary and the end of classical confessionalism at that institution, was an historic turning-point for Reformed theology.

I shall return to Hodge's article later on. What I wish to do in this article is to argue that once again confessional Reformed theology, along with its close relatives of confessional Lutheranism and conservative evangelicalism, stands at a crucial crossroads in its history; and that the opening years of the twenty-first century present the orthodox Christian world in general with a series of serious challenges to its theology and its ecclesiastical identity. I want to make the case that the only hope for such orthodox theology, and for the churches which give visible expression to such theology, lies in the ability – or rather the willingness – of those of us who claim the name Christian to be what we always should be. That is, exponents of a counter-cultural movement which finds its norms and its purpose not in an assimilation to the wider culture but in a recovery of its own distinctiveness.

Anti-Historical Tendencies

The aspect of modern life which I wish to highlight as presenting one of the most significant threats to the Reformed faith is that of the tendency of the modern world to be anti-historical. By this, I mean the aversion of modern men and women to tradition and history as a source of wisdom and even authority. In a world where the very language that is used reflects the deep-seated suspicion of all things old and an adulation of most things new, this is hardly a contentious claim. It is, however, one that has massive significance for the church and for theology.

Before engaging in closer analysis of this problem, we must first acknowledge that it is too easy for those who spend their lives studying ideas and concepts to overestimate the role of self-conscious intellectuals in creating this anti-historical atmosphere. When students, in the rarefied atmosphere of university libraries, read of anti-historical tendencies many instinctively reach for their textbooks of anti-historical philosophies and the primers of deconstructive method. Yet to do so is to expose themselves to the error of seeing the problem of the importance of history merely as a crisis in intellectual method and philosophy. It is certainly to be seen as such in certain contexts. But as so often happens in the history of ideas, a problem that appears to manifest itself as primarily philosophical and intellectual can have roots which lie deep in the wider cultural milieu.

We must be aware that we live in a world where, for most people, designer labels, credit cards and the Pill are of far more immediate and decisive significance than the prison notebooks of Antonio Gramsci or the musings of Michel Foucault. In other words, to understand the world in which we live, we must not only engage in intellectual genealogy in order to establish the philosophical roots of the modern world but we must also broaden our analysis to engage with the wider sociology of

knowledge. Thus what follows will not be confined solely to
the history of ideas as traditionally conceived but will also look
at the broader picture of society.

The intellectual roots of the modern anti-historical tendency
can be found in the Enlightenment of the seventeenth and
eighteenth centuries. Whether one looks at the continental or
the Anglo-American tradition, it is quite clear that the rhetoric
of the new and the novel quickly becomes associated with the
improved and the better. While the last thing a theologian in
the sixteenth century or before wished to be accused of was
novelty or innovation, in the Enlightenment era an iconoclastic
view of history and tradition was seen as part and parcel of the
freeing of humankind from bondage and darkness. Thus, Vol-
taire, Kant and company were happy to understand themselves
as taking part in an 'enlightenment' and surround their work
with the language of liberty, while dismissing their predecessors
as scholastic, obscurantist, and inhabiting the dark ages. This
intellectual tendency toward the exaltation of the new at the
expense of the old was massively reinforced with the advent of
the Industrial Revolution. At this time new modes of production,
urbanisation, and the rise to dominance of the middle classes
led to the fundamental reshaping of society and its values. In
an apocalyptic passage in *The Communist Manifesto*, Karl Marx,
writing in the heat of the Industrial Revolution, describes the
changes he sees around him:

> The bourgeoisie cannot exist without constantly revolutionizing
> the instruments of production, and thereby the relations of pro-
> duction, and with them the whole relations of society.... All fixed,
> fast-frozen relations, with their train of ancient and venerable
> prejudices and opinions, are swept away, all new ones become
> antiquated before they can ossify. All that is solid melts into air,
> all that is holy is profaned, and man is at last compelled to face
> with sober senses his real conditions of life, and his relations with
> his kind.[2]

---

2. Karl Marx, *The Revolutions of 1848: Political Writings I* (London: Penguin,
1973), 70.

Thus the preference of the Enlightenment for the new and the novel at the level of ideas found its social counterpart in the changes driven by the Industrial Revolution, and its concrete expression in the changed economic and social relations in society. All of this militated against the older, classical notion that history and tradition were important sources of positive wisdom.

Looking around today it is quite clear that these anti-historical tendencies have reached something of a climax in the Western societies of the present time. The advanced consumerism of the West promotes novelty as an absolute virtue. Marx would no doubt have seen this as the result of capitalism's need to be constantly creating new products and new markets for itself. One may hesitate to go all the way with the Marxist analysis of the situation in purely material terms but one cannot deny some truth to such an argument. It is, after all, crucial that we do not wear yesterday's fashions, sport yesterday's labels, or listen to yesterday's music lest we be labelled, not so much 'reactionary' as 'square' or 'out of touch'. And who says that this is the case? The people whose financial security depends upon the sale of more and more of their products. In addition, the cult of youth is evident in everything from the domination on television of adverts aimed at young people to the plethora of available anti-ageing products. The underlying ideology would seem to be clear: the young, the fresh, the new is good; the old, the aged, the traditional is bad.

This anti-historical commitment of modern consumerist society finds its ideological counterpart in some of the strands of that amorphous group of philosophies which go under the over-used name of postmodernism. Ever since Marx, Freud, and Nietzsche, secular thinking has been aware of the specious nature of claims to objectivity in all realms, including the historical. Even within a modernist framework the need for a hermeneutic of suspicion in the study of history comes across clearly in the work of a traditional Marxist historian such as Eric Hobsbawm. In the introduction to *The Invention of Tradition* (a collection of essays on the creation and applications of various traditions), along with accompanying spurious historical pedigrees, Hobsbawm notes three overlapping uses of types of tradition since the Industrial Revolution. Some traditions establish or symbolise the social cohesion of certain groups; some establish or legitimise institutions or certain power relations; and some inculcate value systems, patterns of behaviour, and social conventions in the interest of socialisation and social stability.[3] What underlies each of these three types is the manipulation – or even 'creation' – of history and historical narrative for some ulterior political purpose, either of social control or of legitimation.

What is a useful critical tool in the hands of a traditional Marxist becomes an utterly destructive and self-defeating weapon in the hands of those thinkers who have pushed the hermeneutic of suspicion to its logical conclusions. In the world of postmodern history, the point is neither to *reconstruct* the past, as in the work of tradition positivist historians, nor to *construct* it as in the work of traditional Marxists, but rather to *deconstruct* it. It is to lay bare the hidden agendas which underlie all historical narratives and to ask the key question again and again, who owns history?[4] For the ownership of any given historical narrative is intimately linked to the question of who wields power in the present. Hence, the last two decades have seen a ferocious reaction against the traditional narrative of history that focused on Europe and on white heterosexual males. This has been reinforced by a consequent growth in histories from other perspectives, for example those of women, blacks and gays. Perhaps the most famous and articulate exponent of this rejection of traditional history was the late French intellectual, Michel Foucault. As Richard Evans summarises the position of Foucault on history:

---

3. Eric Hobsbawm and Terence Ranger (eds), *The Invention of Tradition* (Cambridge: CUP, 1992), 9.

4. For a survey and discussion of postmodern approaches to history by a historian who is profoundly influenced by Michel Foucault and Hayden White, see Alun Munslow, *Deconstructing History* (London: Routledge, 1997). For a vigorous restatement of a modernist position, see Richard J. Evans, *In Defence of History* (London: Granta, 1997).

History [for Foucault] was a fiction of narrative order imposed on the irreducible chaos of events in the interests of the exercise of power. And if one version of the past was more widely accepted than others, this was not because it was nearer the truth, or conformed more closely to 'the evidence', but because its exponents had more power within the historical profession, or within society in general, than its critics.[5]

For such as Foucault, therefore, histories do not offer explanations of how we come to be where we are in the traditional sense of the word; rather they offer bids for power, attempts to legitimise particular institutions or attitudes in the present. Thus, historical narratives, along with other attempts to provide all-embracing explanations of reality or to make truth-claims, must be unmasked and exposed as the bids for power that they really are. As the Enlightenment downgraded history and tradition by stigmatising them with the language of obscurantism and reaction, and as consumerism has made space for history only as a marketing opportunity in the shape of theme parks and nostalgia shops, so much recent philosophy has labelled history as yet another surreptitious attempt to exert power under the guise of objective truth. Taken together, the voracious appetite for novelty and innovation that marks advanced consumerist societies, and the inveterate cynicism of the modern world, whether expressed in popular political apathy or sophisticated postmodern theories, have proved to be a potent anti-historical, anti-traditional combination.

The Impact on the Church
This article is not intended as a sketch map of contemporary society. The purpose is to address the very serious question of where and how orthodox Christian theology, as classically conceived, can speak to this day and this generation and why, therefore, time should be spent studying it at the start of the third millennium. Before a positive agenda can be offered, however, some time needs to be spent assessing the impact of the

5. Evans, *In Defence of History*, 195-96.

various anti-historical trends, noted above, on the Christian church. If society at large is losing its sense of history, and if the academy is launching a full-frontal assault upon the very possibility of history, how is this affecting the church?

I want to suggest that anti-historical trends of the pragmatic, consumer society of the West have elicited two differing but equally inadequate and, ultimately, anti-historical, responses from the church in the West. First, part of the church has itself enthusiastically embraced these tendencies and has abandoned its self-conscious position within a historical tradition, leaving itself somewhat rootless. Second, part of the church has attempted to grasp the significance of history once again by seeking traditions to enrich its spirituality, but has done this in a manner which is historically fallacious and ultimately a symptom of precisely the same consumerism which has shaped the first response.

To take the first point, the evidence of a collapse in historical rootedness is evident for all to see. We can start by looking at the liturgical practices of the church. By 'liturgical practice' I do not mean specific formal liturgies such as the Book of Common Prayer. Rather I use the term to refer to the broader linguistic and ritualistic shape of Christian worship: the kind of songs that are sung, prayers that are prayed, and sermons that are preached. When looked at in these broad terms, the last twenty or thirty years have seen a veritable transformation of Christian practice, with many churches abandoning traditional hymnody and worship service structures in favour of songs that are more contemporary and service styles that are more conducive to modern sensibilities. More often than not, these changes are implemented with more than a passing reference to the need to attract young people to church – a most legitimate aim but also perhaps a significant modification of the emphases contained in the Great Commission where the category of age receives no specific mention. It is also interesting that a clear connection is being made between attracting youth and breaking decisively with the past in key areas. The ideology of consumerism, with its emphasis on novelty, youth markets etc., clearly lies just below the surface.

To use language that is familiar to a consumer society, no one should make the mistake of seeing the move to contemporary praise songs and service styles as simply a straightforward, value-neutral repackaging or rebranding of a traditional product. After all, at a basic level, language and worship forms offer significant lines of continuity with the past, a past which inevitably shapes our identity in the present. This is seen quite clearly in the Bible's own teaching, whereby the Passover is instituted as a means of commemorating God's mighty act of salvation of ancient Israel. The ceremony was to be repeated annually as a reminder to the Israelites both of what God had done in the past and, consequently, who they were in the present. The historical connection is underlined by the reference in Exodus 12:26-27, where God instructs the Israelites what to say when their children question them about why the Passover is celebrated. The same is true in the Christian church: connection with the past is vital. Of course, the Bible and the sacraments provide us with the basic, vital historical connection to God's saving action in Christ; but there is also a wealth of theological and church tradition which, while not authoritative in the way that Scripture is, is yet extremely useful for maintaining the knowledge of who Christians are, through relating them to the past; and one important avenue for this is the church's current liturgical practices. The language and the practices of the Christian community, tried and tested over the centuries, while not in themselves absolutely sacrosanct, should not be casually abandoned or lightly cast to one side. They are an important element in the identity of the church; and to break decisively with them on the purely pragmatic grounds of enhanced marketablity risks the displacement of the church's historic identity.

Of course, Protestantism has always had the potential of providing fertile soil for a theology and a church culture which disparages tradition. The notion of scriptural authority as ar-

ticulated by the Reformers and by subsequent Reformed and
Lutheran thinkers inevitably subordinated church tradition to
the Bible. It created a situation where tradition could, where
necessary, be abandoned. They regarded the Bible as the sole
source of revelation and that inevitably meant Protestants were
far more critical and selective in their approach to the church's
dogmatic tradition than was typically the case in medieval
Catholicism. Nevertheless the Reformers and the subsequent
tradition never intended this notion of scriptural authority to
act as the means for a wholesale rejection of the church's theological traditions in themselves; they saw it simply as a critical
tool by which those traditions could be continuously critiqued
and reformed.

While there were groups within the sixteenth and seventeenth centuries who argued for just such a rejection of all tradition on the basis of a radical biblicism, it is most significant
that these groups were not part of the magisterial Reformation
and were repudiated by the mainstream. The most famous and
influential of these were the Socinians. The Socinians originated in Italy but flourished in Poland. They rejected even the
doctrines of the Trinity and the Incarnation on the grounds of
a literalist hermeneutic combined with an emphatic rejection
of metaphysics within theology.

Here there are obvious parallels with the sophisticated theo-
logical-historical work of later liberals such as Adolf von Harnack, but at a less sophisticated level the Socinian understanding
of scriptural authority is alive and well within the evangelical
church today, fuelled by the very anti-historical and innovative
forces of modern western consumerism. At the level of ideology,
it can be seen in the work of the so-called 'openness of God'
movement associated with such as Clark Pinnock and Greg Boyd
– a movement which, incidentally, shares significant ground
with the work of von Harnack as well as with early Socinianism
in its opposition to the alleged distorting metaphysics of the orthodox Christian tradition, patristic, medieval and Reformation
on the grounds of a radical scripture principle. Thus, their god

has limited knowledge of the future and continually changes in relation to his creation. Given the amount of metaphysical language deployed in patristic trinitarian discussions, we may well ultimately find that this Socinian approach to theology will place God's trinitarian nature in danger. Maybe this will not happen, but, as this has always been the result of such anti-metaphysical crusades in the past, the omens are not good.

At a more mundane level, the application of this crude scripture principle can be seen in the everyday life and practices of evangelical churches around the world where cries of 'No creed but the Bible', preaching which fails to draw biblical exegesis into theological synthesis, and a disregard for historic patterns of worship and confession, are offered in all seriousness as examples of fidelity to the authority of Scripture. The underlying assumption seems to be that the Protestant notion of scriptural authority can only exist with an iconoclastic attitude to tradition, a position the Reformers themselves would have repudiated. This kind of neo-Socinianism, whether at the level of ideology or of practice, is one response of the church to the challenge of modernity and consumerism.

So much for the first type of church response to modern anti-historical tendencies. The second response is, on the surface at least, almost the exact opposite. This response is that of recovering earlier Christian tradition as a means of rediscovering a more authentic spirituality than the church in the West has generally offered. The most influential example of this in Britain is the so-called rediscovery over the last two decades of Celtic Christianity, the spirituality of the Celtic churches in the early Middle Ages. In a veritable cornucopia of books, the Celtic way has been promoted in church circles as the recovery of a previous lost dimension of church tradition. The Celtic way is promoted as more in tune with nature, as less obsessed with the theme of sin, as offering a spirituality which appeals to the whole person, and as being more rooted in images than in words. All of this is seen as giving it a superior value to that of sin-obsessed Western Augustinianism, particularly as this found its ultimate expression in the word-centred, cerebral religion of the Reformation. The Reformation, as the birthing-room of modernity and Enlightenment, of imperialism, of individualism (whatever that means), and ultimately industrialization, is seen as the ultimate theological disaster and the source of many of the modern world's ills.

Yet this 'Celtic revival', while superficially appearing to represent a return to history and tradition, is on the whole simply a theological manifestation of the same phenomenon we see in society around us. It is an eclectic and nostalgic appropriation of a pseudo-history which supplies the church with a specious historical authenticity. To apply the categories of Hobsbawm, the church, having lost sight of its real historical roots, has invented traditions for the purpose of socialization and legitimation in the present. Within the mythology of the Celtic Christianity movement, the ideal of the Celt functions for today's adherent of Celtic Christianity in a manner similar to that in which the ideal of the 'noble savage' did for the generation of Rousseau.

As to the historical integrity of the movement, this has been exposed as a complete sham in a book by Donald Meek, Professor of Celtic, at Aberdeen University.[6] He points out that none of the high-profile advocates of Celtic spirituality know any of the Celtic languages, and so have no direct access to the sources. He analyses the cultural history of the movement, with its highly selective approach to Celtic matters and exposes it as historical nonsense. Indeed, his work is embarrassing in the way that a badly-matched boxing fight is embarrassing. In the end, one almost feels sorry for his opponents because they have taken such a merciless and effective beating from a man who actually reads the sources and knows the history.

What Meek demonstrates so well is that Celtic Christianity is more akin to the New Age movement in terms of its rejection of the literary in favour of the visual, its obsession with ecological issues, and its desire to reject certain aspects (though by no means all) of Western culture. Indeed, one area where the new

---

6. *The Quest for Celtic Christianity* (Edinburgh: Handsel Press, 2000).

Celtic Christians reveal their Western, consumerist colours so effectively is in the matter of ascetic practices. The rigorous penitential system, which was one of *the* hallmarks uniting Welsh, Scottish and Irish churches, is conspicuous only by its almost total absence from the modern Celtic Christianity movement.[7] Like pampered Hollywood stars who proclaim their adherence to Buddhism, and meditate daily, yet continue to live lives of massive consumption and self-indulgence, most modern Celtic Christians appear to take the bits of the tradition which appeal and leave the rest, unpurchased, on the shelf.

As such, it is scarcely the authentic recovery of historical tradition which it claims to be, but is rather the invention of tradition by a culture which finds itself rootless and disillusioned. Such a culture needs to invent a history for itself that will meet its contemporary concerns. It is, therefore, only superficially different from the outright rejection of tradition that can be seen in many evangelical quarters. It uses language, names and symbols which would appear to give it historical integrity; yet it does so in a manner that is driven not by the sources but by the romantic vision of certain people in the modern world.

In sketch form this is the Western European world of today. Christianity is no longer the dominant cultural force which it once was; in other words, we live in a post-Christian pluralistic society. The church itself has in large part abandoned its historic pedigree, as is evidenced by the worship songs that are sung, by the kind of things spoken in church, and by the widespread ignorance of church history and tradition. Furthermore, where tradition is held in high esteem, as in the Celtic Christianity movement, it is often done in a way that is both self-consciously iconoclastic towards the Western tradition in general and the Reformation tradition in particular. With this in mind some will ask: why study orthodox, historic Christian theology, particularly in its classical Reformed form, at the start of the third millennium? I would like to reply to this by proposing

7. See Meek, 95 ff.

two theses.

Thesis One: the Reformed tradition takes seriously the biblical teaching that God is primarily a speaking God.

It almost goes without saying that the Reformed church originated in a movement of words. The Bible translations, the pamphlets, the sermons, and even the changes to church architecture which the Reformed church embodied, all speak volumes about the increasing significance of words in the sixteenth and seventeenth centuries. While social and cultural historians would no doubt root this in a complex of historical forces, from the invention of the printing press to rising literacy rates, burgeoning trade, changing fiscal policies, and increases in bureaucracy and record-keeping, for those who take self-understanding and even theology seriously as categories of significance to historians, the conviction among the Reformed, that God is a God who speaks, must also be allowed to play its part in the analysis. The importance of the notions of command and, above all, promise to the Protestant message immediately meant that Protestantism was inevitably going to be an irreducibly verbal phenomenon. One simply cannot command or promise by mere symbols, as was made so clear in the Reformers' insistence that the sacraments could not be administered except in the congregation and in the context of the clear and comprehensible preaching of the Word.

In addition to this very obvious point, we might also make reference to the careful articulation of the relationship between the Word of God conceived as the second person of the Trinity, and the Word of God as Scripture, both of which identifications are commonplace in Reformed theology. The emphasis upon God the Father working by the Word through the Holy Spirit as the ontic source of our knowledge of God was not seen as standing in any way opposed to the emphasis on the inscripturated Word as the cognitive ground for theology. God and words were thus theologically inseparable in the Reformed account of revelation. This simple point finds biblical warrant in the consistent scriptural testimony to God as the God who speaks, who uses words in order to address humankind and to reveal himself to humankind, whether in the context of Mount Sinai or of the Mount of Olives. The Christian God is the God who speaks, who communicates and relates to his people in a manner which is inextricably bound up with speech and with words.

At this point it is necessary to highlight two current trends, one broadly cultural, the other more narrowly intellectual, which strike at the very heart of this notion of a speaking God. The first is the general shift within our culture from the literary or the verbal to the visual and the iconic. As the Reformation, and the Reformed theology which it nurtured, were in part the products of a cultural shift from the visual to the verbal, we now stand at a point in history where the cultural pendulum is swinging back somewhat in the opposite direction. While the sixteenth century had its printing press and its book industry, today there is television and, more recently, the internet. While it is true that these latter media involve words and language, the emphasis or the dominant mode of communication within both is that of the visual image. To give examples is easy: one can cite the US presidential debate between Kennedy and Nixon in 1960, where radio listeners thought Nixon had won while television viewers gave the result to Kennedy. The reason? Kennedy *looked* cool, suntanned and physically prepossessing while Nixon, although he *sounded* more impressive, was pale and gaunt, having just returned from hospital. If the television could exert such ominous power in 1960, how much more significant is it today, in a world where the most powerful men and women in the world are, with little doubt, those who control the giant global television industry.

This cultural shift raises huge questions for the church and for theology. For a start, the church has to face the perennial question of how its message can be communicated in the surrounding culture. Such a question has always involved some form of dialogue with and accommodation to the wider context, even if, for some, this has only meant that the word must be preached in a language society can understand. The major question that is posed by our increasingly visual culture is: can the gospel be communicated in a more visual manner?

There are many who answer yes to this question – and do so with an unnerving passion. To return to the interest in Celtic spirituality, this is a movement that lays far more stress upon the emotions and upon symbols and aesthetics than upon the intellect and dogma. It is the classic spirituality for the visual age, with its mysticism, its artwork and its disdain for classic doctrinal formulations. But it is not Celtic spirituality that needs to be focused on here. What we need to be concerned about is the replacement of preaching and doctrine in many generic evangelical churches with drama, with so-called liturgical dance, with feelings, emotions and mystical experiences, and, sometimes, with elaborate sacramental ceremonies which make the Catholic Church look positively Puritan by comparison. These all speak of the transformation of Protestantism from a word-based movement into something more concerned with aesthetics of one form or another.

This is where a thorough grounding in the classic Reformed or evangelical faith is so important at the level of church leadership. If the central notion of the God who speaks is more than simply a social construct, an act of cultural projectionism, then the movement against words in the church – whether words in preaching, prayer, or doctrine – is a movement with profound theological implications. It is not simply a rebellion against words in themselves: it is also a rebellion against the God who speaks them. Yet it seems that the argument is being won within the churches by the advocates of the new aesthetic Protestantism almost by default. Of all the forms of Protestantism to emerge from the Reformation, that of the Reformed tradition is the one which reflected at most length upon the notion of the God who speaks and worked out the implications of this for the church's theology and practice. It is thus crucial at this time that the Reformed church should take the lead in critiquing current aesthetic trends within evangelicalism and reasserting once more the centrality of God and of God's speech to the church at large. I would suggest that Reformed theology, with its rich tradition of careful reflection upon the notion of the God who speaks, is superbly placed to address these issues with the seriousness and the biblical fidelity which they demand.

The war against words, however, is not simply being conducted at the level of popular cultural trends. It has also received significant intellectual expression in the various schools of literary criticism and social science which emerged from France in the 1960s and which now hold sway within many universities and seminaries in Europe and North America. While any generalised description of these schools is bound to be simplistic, it is accurate to say that one characteristic which many share is the notion that meaning is ultimately determined by the reader or reading community and not by the author or the texts themselves. The so-called 'death of the author' is something one sees frequently trumpeted from the lecterns of lecture theatres, books of literary theory, and the pages of influential literary journals.

In a significant study of such theories from a Christian point of view, Kevin Vanhoozer has argued that the death of God in the sixties became the death of the author in the nineties. In other words, he sees the attack on the authority of authors and texts as being, at root, a theological problem, a rebellion against God. Certainly, the case seems compelling. If Dostoevsky was correct in seeing the non-existence of God as thrusting man into the abyss of ethical nihilism, then Vanhoozer would seem to be correct in seeing the death of God as thrusting man into the abyss of epistemological nihilism. In other words, the speaking God is that which gives meaning to all life, whether it be moral codes or texts.[8]

Once again, this is where the Reformed faith is singularly well placed to meet the challenge. While there is considerable evidence that many within the broader evangelical constituency are flirting with aspects of postmodern literary theory, though often in a highly derivative and simplified form, Vanhoozer's warning ought to be heeded. While the days when the meaning

---

8. See Kevin Vanhoozer, *Is There a Meaning in This Text?* (Leicester: Apollos, 1998).

of texts could be regarded as generally clear and self-evident is long gone – and the Reformed, with their understanding of the epistemological impact of sin should have no problem with this idea – the notion that communities or readers create meaning is highly dangerous and ultimately thrusts God back into the realm of the noumenal, incapable of communicating with his people. Once again, it is here that the Reformed emphasis upon the God who speaks to humanity, the God who accommodates himself to human capacity, is counter-cultural in terms of wider trends but also crucial in terms of the future survival of the church. Christians have a God who speaks; and that has profound implications for the manner in which they are able to interact with and appropriate contemporary trends in epistemology.

Thesis Two: The Reformed Faith appreciates the beneficial aspects of history and tradition.

The suspicion and disdain that characterises much of the modern attitude to history and tradition was noted above. At the level of mass culture, the impact of consumerism as generating a continual need for the new and the novel was noted. At the level of philosophy, a brief look was given at the approach to history of those such as Michel Foucault, who regard the writing of history as being about power and manipulation, in the present as much as in the past, rather than about being a quest for the 'truth', whatever that might be.

There is a level at which the Reformed can agree with such as Foucault. The emphasis in the confessional documents upon total depravity should alert the church to the fact that history and tradition, like everything else, can be written, manipulated, and used in a manner which is profoundly abusive.[9] Indeed, there is a sense in which one could read Foucault's writing as perhaps the greatest reflection upon the significance of total depravity for

---

9. By 'total depravity' I do not mean that everybody is as bad as they possibly can be but that every aspect of humanity is corrupted to some degree by the Fall. Thus, epistemology becomes in part a moral issue and all claims to mere, absolute objectivity are rendered false.

historical writing that there is. Where Foucault errs, along with many Marxists, is in his failure to see that history and tradition can also be profoundly helpful, even liberating, to humanity. The assumption of Foucault is that all history is about power, about classifying and marginalising, about promoting a 'them' and 'us' mentality that is based upon power relations. For Marxists, tradition and history are too often ways of cultivating false consciousness, of maintaining class distinctions and therefore of keeping the poor in their subordinate position in the economic food-chain. For both Foucault and Marxists, therefore, it is imperative to unmask the hidden and manipulative agendas that underlie the writing of the history of the maintenance of traditions. Christians too should be in the game of unmasking the ungodly agendas and bids for power that lurk around every corner – even, or perhaps, especially, in the church; but they must also be aware that, as Christians, their attitude to history should be more nuanced than Foucault and company.

First, they must question the blanket assumption that is found in this kind of secular philosophy that all history and tradition is, by definition, manipulative and abusive. This can be done indirectly by applying the same yardstick to the Marxists and the disciples of Foucault as they apply to others. They could be charged with writing history that is simply ideology dressed up as truth, that is subtly manipulative, that simply marginalises and disenfranchises those whom they wish to subjugate for their own ends; but they would probably have little difficulty agreeing with this claim and little would have been achieved beyond showing the futile nihilism of these approaches when consistently applied across the board. Relativising the relativisers ultimately calls forth cries of little more than 'So what?' from those watching on the sidelines. Far better to point to the profoundly disorienting cultural and social effects which the collapse of history and tradition have brought in their wake in recent years. As historical ignorance and anti-traditionalism have increased with the rise of Western consumerism, society has not witnessed any great liberation; rather, there has been the creation of a desperate and deep-seated craving for precisely the kind of identity which history and tradition are capable of supplying. Thus, for example, we have the rise of new, militant nationalisms and the invention of the pseudo-historical New Age spiritualities. The removal and destruction of traditions and histories which actually have some roots in the real past has frequently not liberated humanity but rather left aching voids which have been filled with synthetic traditions and histories which are indeed truly the invention of those who promote them; and arguably these have proved far more manipulative than many which have gone before.[10] Multinational consumerism reduces all of life to a bland and rootless present, and as humanity finds itself free-floating and rootless, it desperately strives to create (rather than rediscover) for itself a history and a network of tradition which will give it value and identity. The death of history and the death of tradition has not proved to be a liberating experience; it has merely created a hole into which any old fairy-story can now be fitted.

The first reason for the importance of the study of the Reformed faith in this context is, therefore, that it does provide the church with a history and a tradition upon which to build its identity and understand its place in the wider world. The Reformed church, with its creeds, confessions, catechisms, and theological tradition, provides its people with the historical continuity that so many crave today, and that is so crucial if they are not to be blown here and there by every puff of doctrine or every passing fad. Unlike alternative traditions, such as that of Celtic spirituality, however, our tradition is defined by public documents, creeds, confessions, and historical movements, not by romantic speculation about what might have happened, speculation which speaks more of contemporary aspirations than actions in real time-space history. Of course, the past can be romanticised and people can become idolatrous with regard

---

10. Along similar lines, though from an avowedly Marxist perspective, Terry Eagleton has criticised postmodernism precisely on the grounds that it is profoundly politically disempowering: see Terry Eagleton, *The Illusions of Postmodernism* (Oxford: Blackwell, 1996).

to traditions. This is a most serious and ever-present danger, and one has only to think of the way that the Reformed faith has been used in the past to realise that it can as easily be a means of oppression as of liberation. However, the danger at this particular point in time would seem to be that of thoughtless iconoclasm than of rampant idolatry. This is not to say that the church is simply in the business of maintaining its tradition for the sake of tradition and of accepting uncritically all that the tradition contains. That would be to raise tradition to the level of revelation, the very thing against which our Reformation forefathers reacted so strongly. It is rather to argue that our tradition provides us with a place to stand and a starting-point from which we can assess the world around us, ourselves, and even aspects of our tradition itself. By so doing, we can acknowledge in all humility that, while the church in the past may indeed have made mistakes, informed reflection on that past is nevertheless crucial to any intelligent engagement with the present. I would suggest that the critical appropriation of church tradition that we see in the best theologians of the sixteenth and seventeenth centuries in fact provides a fine model of how to relate to history and tradition today.

This is also where the catholicity of the Reformed faith offers great opportunities. A careful reading of the great Reformed theologians of the past indicates that Reformed thought is far from sectarian in its spirit. The great trinitarian creeds of the early church provide the backdrop to the tradition; and those theologians who lie behind the confessional standards of the sixteenth and seventeenth centuries, while standing firm on their beliefs and adamantly refusing to reduce all doctrine to the level of adiaphora, yet interacted with all shades of theological opinion and still provide both a theology and a pattern of engagement which seeks to do justice to the wider theological scene in a manner which is articulate rather than obscurantist. An appreciation of history, and of the doctrinal struggles of the church throughout history, are surely crucial to the avoidance of a narrow sectarianism and self-righteousness in the present. If the church capitulates to the anti-historical forces at work around us, it is exposed to all manner of unfortunate consequences, not least the potential of repeating many of the theological errors of the past.

While this is to argue for the general usefulness of history and tradition, note must also be taken of the fact that, for the Reformed, the problem with the relentless assault on history and tradition, at both intellectual and popular levels, also has a profound theological dimension. Our understanding of God is that he is a God who works through history, and whose identity and purposes are bound up with the way he has acted in times past. This is an important biblical truth, as any number of refer-ences in the Pentateuch, the Psalms, the Prophets or the New Testament tell us. We can neither simply accept the radical approach to history and tradition that reduces it all to the level of a power struggle, nor can we opt for the innovative and crea-tive approach that is found in Celtic spirituality, which simply creates the past it wishes to discover. History means something because God is its author; at root, the attacks on history from both the academy and modern popular culture are profoundly theological because they are attempts once again to push God out of the big picture. They may not deny his existence; but they effectively deny him any positive relation with his creation. That is at best Deism.

This is why Reformed theology is so important. With the centrality of the notion of covenant to its theological scheme, the Reformed faith places the God who works in history right at the heart of its confession. At the level of theology, this is surely as crucial to holding the Bible together as a theological unity as is the notion of the one God who speaks in the Bible. It is one of the strengths of Reformed theology that it sees the biblical history as witnessing to the actions of a single God who is committed to the salvation of his people through the Messiah who marks the culmination of the history of his covenant people. While there are manifest problems in extending this approach to our reading of post-biblical history, the notion of covenant, the place of families and children within our understanding of the church, and the centrality of the sacraments to our worship,

all reinforce the importance of continuity with God's saving actions throughout history. As soon as sight is lost of this historical
dimension to God's action, then there will be a tendency towards
mysticism and individualism and all sight is lost of the real significance of the church as the covenant community of the God
who rules over history and works within history. We will also
lose sight of the importance of theological and practical humility in the Christian life: so much of today's attitude to the past
is iconoclastic; so little of it reflects the attitude of people like
Paul in the Pastoral letters. Acknowledging that God works in
history means that we acknowledge that he has worked in the
past; and acknowledging that he has worked in the past means
that we acknowledge that we may not ignore that past as if we
today had all the answers.

In short, without God as its author, history becomes meaningless, as do the lives of all those who make up history. All that is
left is the unchained and autonomous individual in the present.
The way we worship becomes whatever suits us here and now;
and our theology becomes whatever we think the Bible means
or whatever the latest scholarly consensus tells us it means. In
short, we lose any perspective from which to be self-critical.

We might add, finally, that when we lose sight of God's work
in the past we may easily also lose sight of his work in the future,
of the eschatological dimension of the Christian faith. Once we
neglect the past, we will also just as surely fail to understand the
significance of the present in relation to the future. This is one of
the reasons why many evangelical churches have an over-realised
eschatology. The failure to understand the significance of history
in God's purposes has led to a failure to understand the balance
that exists in the Bible regarding the now/not yet tension in
relation to the coming of the kingdom. This provides fertile soil
for, at the trivial level, nothing but triumphalist worship songs
with no room for Christian suffering, and, at the more openly
dubious level, prosperity teaching, total healing movements,
and all manner of groups who fail to come to real grips with the
reality and the problem of evil in the present day. Such over-
realised eschatology is itself another function of a consumerist,

credit-card culture that wants everything now, and will not
wait until tomorrow. The disastrous pastoral consequences of
such teaching, not to mention its theological inadequacies, are
visible round about for all to see. By contrast, Reformed theology, by giving due place to history in God's purposes, points
beyond the present to a brighter future in eschatological glory
and thus does justice to the biblical tension involved in living
in the world between Pentecost and the Parousia.

Why, then, should we study the Reformed faith today? The
answer is because it offers the most effective and biblical anti-
dote to the forces around us which most threaten Christianity.
These are Western materialist consumerism and its concomitant
ideologies of the superiority of the new and the rejection of the
old. The cultural war around us is, at a very deep level, a war
against history and thus against the God who works in and
through history. In this context, the Reformed faith sets forth
the theological importance of history with supreme clarity; it
also offers us a framework for doing justice not just to biblical
history but also to church tradition.

Times are hard for Reformed traditionalists, not least because
of precisely this current questioning of the value of history. But
they should not lose heart – if God has worked in the past, then
he will work in the present and in the future. I thus leave the
last words to Caspar Wistar Hodge, who concluded the essay
alluded to earlier in the following way:

> [T]hough in theological circles and in ecclesiastical courts the lead-
> ers of Reformed thought find scant recognition, wherever humble
> souls catch the vision of God in His glory and bow in humility and
> adoration before Him, trusting for salvation only in His grace and
> power, there you have the essence of the Reformed Faith, and God
> in His providence may yet raise up a leader of religious thought
> who shall once again make the Reformed Faith a power in the
> theological world. If and when this happens we may confidently

---

11. C. W. Hodge (1929), 'The Reformed Faith,' *Evangelical Quarterly*, 3-24,
23-24.

TWO

THE UNDOING OF THE REFORMATION?

A Significant Cultural Shift

One of the most significant events in the post-war world took place in 1960. It was an early example of what is now so commonplace as to pass without note or comment, yet what it indicated about the change taking place within Western culture was little short of earth-shattering. I refer, of course, to the pre-election presidential debate between the Democratic nominee, John F. Kennedy, and his Republican rival, Richard M. Nixon. The debate itself was unremarkable – it was fairly standard election fare – unremarkable, that is, except for one fascinating and significant outcome: those who heard the discussion on radio thought that Nixon had won; but those who watched on television were convinced that it was Kennedy, not Nixon, who emerged as victor. The reason? On radio, the sharp debating skills of the Republican placed him in the driving seat; but on television, Nixon, recently released from hospital, looked exhausted and haggard, and cut a sorry figure by the side of the tanned, relaxed, vibrant-looking Kennedy. That the latter won hands down on television was a graphic signal that the modern televisual age had truly arrived.

What this event in 1960 indicated was happening has, since that time, become a seismic shift in the nature of our culture. More and more it is the image, the visual, that commands power: from the heartbreaking pictures of bomb victims in Northern Ireland and starving millions in Africa to the trivial glamour of film stars and popular musicians, the world of today is dominated by images and icons.

The most obvious sign of this phenomenon is that the focal point of real power in the modern world is the media, particularly the predominantly visual media of television and the tabloid newspapers. Indeed, the following comment of Marshall

McLuhan on the Vietnam War expresses succinctly the sheer power of the television in today's world:

> Television brought the brutality of war into the comfort of the living room. Vietnam was lost in the living rooms of America, not on the battlefields of Vietnam.[1]

It is hardly surprising, then, that the most powerful men and women in the world today are probably not the politicians, but media moguls such as Rupert Murdoch and Ted Turner. Politicians, after all, depend for their very survival upon the goodwill of the media, particularly television. Clinton only escaped the Lewinsky debacle at the end of the day because the media decided to cast Kenneth Starr as the villain; the British monarchy only survived (sadly) as it did in the aftermath of Princess Diana's death because the media decided to call off the packhounds; and, while the Tories were without doubt on their way out of office in 1997, perhaps Tony Blair only won the election that year with as huge a majority as he did because he had managed to gain the support of Rupert Murdoch for his cause (let us not forget the visit he made to Murdoch in the run-up to the election, or the crucial role of *The Sun* in the equally remarkable victory of John Major in 1992). In addition, one has only to look at the billions of dollars and pounds spent on advertising to see where 'the market', that infallible judge of what is and is not important in contemporary society, regards the centres of power to be: advertising, TV air-time, and image/PR consultancies whose sole reason for existence is the manipulation or 'spinning' of the media to a client's advantage. The visual media (whether of the televisual or of the tabloid newspaper variety), with all the associated baggage of 'spin doctors', PR people etc, is without doubt one of the dominant forces within our culture today, and this has led to a general cultural bias in favour of the visual over and against the verbal.[2] Thus, in entertainment, television

---

1. *Montreal Gazette*, 16 May 1975.

2. For an interesting discussion of this, see Neil Postman, *Amusing Ourselves to Death* (London: Methuen, 1987).

is more popular than radio; and in politics it is more important to look good than to articulate a coherent argument.[3]

Anyone who needs convincing of the power of the visual media, and particularly television, should spend some time reflecting on the way in which it has proved able over the years to control people's thinking to such an extent that it has frequently been able to blur the boundaries between fact and fantasy, truth and reality. There are some obvious examples: the recent advertising campaign for the popular soap-opera *Eastenders* carried the slogan 'Everybody's talking about it', and portrayed normal people, in various ordinary situations, talking about the programme's characters and events as if they were real. It might appear silly – but anyone who has stood for any time in a queue at a bus-stop or supermarket till can vouch for the fact that such conversations are everyday occurrences and that soap characters are spoken about in ways that indicate they are more 'real' to many people than some important politicians and public figures. Indeed, when questions are asked in the House of Commons concerning the wrongful imprisonment of a character on *Coronation Street*, the best we can say is that public money is being crassly wasted (though with the apparent amusement and approval of the general public, at least as refracted through the media); at worst, we have a serious crisis in distinguishing between what is real and what is not, between what is important and what is utterly trivial.

A more dramatic, and in many ways more worrying, example of this fantasy world created by television was, of course, the Diana phenomenon. The scenes of mass hysteria following the tragic death of a young mother were simply incredible – but what was really disturbing, if not a little frightening, was the language of familiarity which so many of the mourners inter-

---

3. Strange to tell, as I was writing this article, a national newspaper carried as a brief news item the story that the Libyan leader, Colonel Gadaffi, has hired a London public relations company to help improve his public image. It would seem that in today's world not even dictators can afford to ignore their public image: see *The Scotsman*, 28 August 1999.

viewed on television used in connection with the dead princess.
'She was a friend to us all'; 'We felt she was one of our own';
'She was like a big sister to me'. Statements like this abounded,
statements which implied that a real, personal relationship existed between Princess Diana and those being interviewed. Such
was not the case: these individuals had come to know an image,
albeit a carefully cultivated image, of a young woman they had
never met but who entered their houses and their lives through
the box of electronic wizardry in the corner of their living room.
Then, at a moment of tragedy for the Princess and her close family and friends, these unknowns had also been swept up in the
death and been bereaved – not of a real friend, but of an image,
of a character in a fantasy world. That they were incapable of
discerning the difference is perhaps the most eloquent testimony
to the power of television in our time.[4]

Paralleling the rise of the television-driven visual culture has
been the collapse in confidence in language. In the academic
sphere, this has manifested itself most dramatically in much
of the modern linguistic philosophy which was pioneered by
French intellectuals in the sixties and seventies, and taken up
with something of a vengeance by British and American social
scientists in the eighties and nineties.[5] While there are a variety

---

4. As a postscript, one might add that the collapse of interest in Diana
witnessed by the increasing public apathy towards the anniversary of the
accident indicates just how superficial the emotions involved in the original
phenomena were, and how swiftly people can recover from tragedies in their
fantasy worlds – as swiftly, indeed, as characters in soap operas routinely
recover from the most horrendous personal misfortunes.

5. The literature in this field is vast. The movements to which I refer are
most commonly associated with the work of Michel Foucault, Jacques Derrida, and the later writings of Roland Barthes; in America, Stanley Fish, Professor at Duke University, has perhaps been most prominent in propagating
literary deconstruction. For a popular survey of the issues from a Christian
perspective, see D. A. Carson, *The Gagging of God: Christianity Confronts Pluralism*
(Leicester: Apollos, 1996). An entertaining – though, from the deconstruc-
tionist perspective, an ultimately unpersuasive – response to postmodernism
from the scientific community is Alain Sokal and Jean Bricmont, *Intellectual
Impostures: Postmodern Philosophers' Abuse of Science* (London: Profile Books,

of 'postmodernisms' on offer, some features are common to al-most all philosophies covered by the umbrella term: the rejection of all-embracing 'metanarratives' which provide comprehensive accounts of reality; a rejection of the idea that language texts can convey a stable meaning (in effect, a denial that authorial intent is of any significance in understanding a text's meaning, the assertion of the so-called 'death of the author'); and a deep suspicion of the motives that underlie any given text. Written texts become not so much means of communication or build-ing relationships; they become battle-grounds for asserting one's own power over another, or one community's power over another, through the privileging or imposition of one's own interpretation over against that of others. In such a universe, evangelical theology is not biblical in the sense that it reflects the mind of God expressed in scripture; it is 'biblical' in that it represents the imposition of one group's particular interpreta-tion on the Bible as a means of defining itself over and against others and of excluding or oppressing those others, be they ethnic minorities, liberals, working class etc.

While these kinds of theories have been, to a large extent, the glass-bead games of a few intellectuals, the parallels with what is happening in the wider world are quite striking. Tele-vision chat shows indicate the existence of a world which has never heard of Jacques Derrida yet where issues of morality and knowledge are decided on the basis of which individual or group is able to put its own agenda across with most persuasive power or, sometimes, most brute force; and such power and force, on chat shows at least (and we must not underestimate the power of these and similar phenomena in shaping opinion), are more often a function rather of the image projected, of the position of the cameras, of the seating of the guests, of the careful editing,

1998). This contains the account and text of the highly amusing 'hermeneutics of quantum gravity' hoax' – an excellent parody of the pretentious verbal garbage of too many critical theorists. Sharp criticism from within the literary establishment comes from Terry Eagleton: see his *The Illusions of Postmodernism* (Oxford: Blackwell, 1996) and *After Theory* (London: Penguin, 2003).

than of the intrinsic merits or demerits of any particular view-
point. Here then, we have the confluence of the visually-driven
nature of our culture with the radical relativism induced by the
popular impact of postmodernism. Indeed, the subordination
of language to image and the rise of deconstruction and critical
theory are surely not unrelated phenomena: both form part of
what one might call the long war against words.

The rise to a position of cultural dominance by the visual
media and the parallel widespread collapse in confidence in
language has its corollary in the various quests to find 'truth'
elsewhere and in other forms – in the visual and the aesthetic,
in the whole realm of experience as opposed to cognition or
intellectual activity. In the religious sphere, the aesthetic is gaining ground against the cerebral. The rise of New Age religion
and Celtic spirituality are just two religious phenomena which
place less emphasis upon doctrine and dogma and more upon
the visual and aesthetic aspects of worship. Even in evangelical
circles, the relentless attack on 'propositional' revelation and
the constant cries for new models of truth, which one hears
from certain quarters, would seem symptomatic of the impact
of the general cultural scene upon theology. To the extent that
such appeals are rooted in an uncritical absorption of some of
the philosophical premises of secular philosophy, to that extent
they would seem to be just the latest examples of evangelical
worldliness.

Given the evident power of the visual and the comparative
weakness of the verbal in contemporary society, what I want to
offer here is an analysis of the situation which sets these phenomena in biblical perspective. The evangelical world, of course,
is full of trendy sociological studies and obfuscatory jargon, and
it is not my intention to contribute to the kind of intellectual
narcissism which so much of this represents. Instead, I want to
indicate what the theological implications of this cultural shift
to the visual are, and to make the case that those evangelicals
who, for the best reasons in the world, seek uncritically to adapt
their theological endeavours, evangelism, and church life to the

norms of the modern, visual/aesthetic society, are making a potentially very serious mistake. The turn – or, rather, the return – to the visual and the aesthetic is, I will argue, ultimately a theological act with profound theological implications.

A Biblical View of Language

From what has been said above, it is clear that the current cultural climate poses a number of significant questions to evangelical theology which the church must answer if it is to continue to be an effective force in the world in which it seeks to witness. For example, in a world where words now have only secondary importance, can the traditional emphasis on words – the Bible, preaching, etc. – be maintained or should it not rather give way to something else, some other means of communicating the message? The importance of contextualisation in cross-cultural contexts is now widely accepted and hardly controversial: should the same approach perhaps not be radically applied to the overall word-based nature of evangelical theology in order to produce something very different in form but more suited to a visual culture? Then, with the trivialisation of reality which the televisual culture seems to inculcate, how is the church to gain an audience and then to impress on that audience the urgency of its message? Unless the church can give a reasoned answer to questions such as these, its future effectiveness will be minimal.

Of course, I have neither the time nor the space to deal comprehensively with these issues here. What I wish to do, however, is to lay the foundations for understanding what is taking place in our culture from a theological perspective. One could give various social, economic, psychological, and technological accounts of the phenomena outlined above, and all would be of some use; of most importance, however, is the theological account, as it is this which will ultimately determine the essence of the church's response.

At heart, the phenomena outlined above are issues of language: the rise of televisual culture has led to the subordination

of language to the visual image; the PR/'spin doctor' industry
is based upon the careful manipulation of language to achieve
certain ends through the creation of a certain image which can
be passed off as reality; and the postmodernism of Derrida and
company is concerned with exposing the real interests that
lie behind the interpretation of language and texts which in
themselves have no fixed meaning. For the church to mount a
suitable response, therefore, it is important first to understand
the importance of language from a biblical perspective.

To put the biblical matter in a nutshell, language in the Bible
is the basis of interpersonal relationships. Creation, of course,
is a highly mysterious event, but it is significant that the Bible
uses the language of speech to express the creative activity of
God. In Genesis 1 and 2, God is the one who converses, speaks,
within himself, and the act of creation arises out of precisely
this kind of interpersonal conversation between the members
of the Trinity. Then, in the Garden of Eden, God's relationship
with Adam is expressed via the medium of language. It is how
God defines the nature and limits of the relationship, and, after
the Fall, it is how God confronts Adam and Eve with their sin.
The same pattern is repeated throughout the whole Bible in
both testaments: whether it is command or promise, the two
basic aspects of the divine-human relationship, God speaks
using words to define his relationship with men and women,
to limit it, to move it forward: he speaks to Noah, to Abraham,
to Samuel, to David and so on. Indeed, God's use of language
is the basic element which allows the encounter between God
and humanity to be considered as a personal relationship. As
Carl Henry says:

> The biblical view implies that God instituted language as a vehicle
> for interpersonal communication and fellowship. In relationships
> with mankind he voluntarily employs language as a divine accom-
> modation. Language enables us to objectify and to communicate
> our thoughts and knowledge claims, as well as our emotions,
> desires and fantasies. It is impossible to see how human culture
> would be possible without it. Yet language was divinely gifted

not primarily to provide a basis for culture, but rather to facilitate intelligible communion between man and God and communication of the truth.[6]

This function of language, of words, grammar, syntax, and sentences as being of the essence of interpersonal relationships, is reinforced by the account of the Tower of Babel. When faced with all-surpassing pride and arrogance of fallen humanity, what is it that God does in order to disrupt human relationships to the point where such an ambitious scheme could never be attempted again? He creates linguistic confusion so that that which is central to human relationships – clear linguistic communication – is utterly disrupted. From that point on, relationships between humans will be severely limited precisely because of the loss of common linguistic currency. Then, of course, as if the biblical view of the importance of the incident at Babel in particular and of language in general needed any further underlining, we have the incident at Pentecost, when the gift of languages is given so that the gospel can be heard and understood by the cosmopolitan crowd in Jerusalem. While the Bible itself makes no explicit connection between the two events (and the plurality of languages clearly remains at Pentecost) the event is highly suggestive: the disruption at Babel, caused by human sin and the subsequent confusion of languages, is overcome in Christ through the work of the Holy Spirit. The relationships between God and humanity, and between individual human beings, are healed and restored in the context of salvation in Christ and expressed in terms of the overcoming of linguistic confusion.

Of course, in saying all this I am not attempting to argue that words are the only way in which the Bible expresses the reality of the relationship between God and humanity. The role of God's presence (or absence) is also a key category in this regard. Nor is language the only way in which God communicates to humanity. The elaborate sacrificial system of the Old Testament, the use by

---

6. Carl F. H. Henry, *God, Revelation and Authority*, 6 vols. (Carlisle: Paternoster, 1999), III, p. 387.

many of the prophets of dramatic incidents to emphasise their message, the miracles of Christ himself, and the ordinances of baptism and the Lord's Supper, all demonstrate the divine use of visual and other aesthetic media for communication between God and humanity. What is important to grasp, however, is that the fundamental significance of all of God's actions in these contexts ultimately requires expression in a verbalised form, often in the categories of command and of promise. The presence or absence of God is always related to obedience or disobedience to the commands of God; and the sacrificial system, the dramatics of the prophets, Christ's miracles, and baptism and the Lord's Supper are all attached at some level to God's commands and promises. In each case, words and sentences give the actions their true theological meaning. Indeed, it is not without significance that Moses tells the Israelites that, when their children ask them about the Passover, they are not simply to perform it but to tell the story of the Israelites' flight from Egypt. The Passover, like the sacrificial system and Christ's miracles, is not in itself its own interpretation: it requires a verbal explanation to draw out its significance. Words are thus of vital importance to biblical religion, even where signs, events, and symbols may be regarded as having a crucial role.

The Reformation as the Recovery of the Theological Importance of Words

Given the biblical importance of language as of the essence of human relationships and, more importantly, of God's relationship with humanity, I would like to argue that it is possible to interpret the theological impact of the Reformation of the sixteenth century as, from one perspective, a recovery of the biblical centrality of words. While many theological perspectives for interpreting the Reformation might suggest themselves – the issue of assurance, the recovery of justification by faith, the emphasis on scripture alone etc. – the theological role assigned to words by the Reformation is, I believe, of perhaps most pressing significance for us today.

The importance of words in the Reformation is, of course, well known. The role of vernacular scriptures and church services was central to the project as a whole, as the work of William Tyndale in England and Martin Luther in Saxony, among others, amply demonstrates. Everywhere the Reformation made an impact, it did so via the production and proliferation of vernacular scriptures and the preaching (i.e., the verbal proclamation) of the Word of God. Perhaps the most graphic sign of the shift from the sacramental emphasis of medieval Catholicism to the Word-based emphasis of the Reformers was the change in church architecture. Enter any great medieval cathedral and one is likely to be struck by the way in which the design focuses attention on the elaborate altar structure; enter somewhere like St. Giles' Cathedral in Edinburgh, however, and the most striking thing is the way in which the raised pulpit is central, with the chairs arranged on all sides, looking inwards. The reason? Church architecture focuses attention on what is the most important part of the church service: in medieval Catholicism, the Mass was central; in Reformation Protestantism, the preaching of the Word was central. In each case, church design simply reflected the underlying ideology. This is not to argue that preaching played no role in medieval Catholicism, nor the sacraments in Reformation Protestantism; but it is to make a highly significant point about emphases and priorities, one that lies at the heart of the difference between the two theological trajectories.

The Word-oriented theology of the Reformation stands within a broader movement in Western Europe to a word-oriented culture. The invention of the printing press in the fifteenth century had led to cheaper books and had fuelled rising literacy rates, with the result that print became the dominant medium of influence at the time. As a result, books and pamphlets became the basic means of spreading Reformation ideas on the international stage. Indeed, so close was the relationship between printing and Reformation that a reductionist historian might well be tempted to view the latter as being essentially a footnote in the history of the former. To do so, however, would certainly not do justice to the intention of the Reformers. For them, the connection between their theology and the medium of disseminating that theology was not an arbitrary contrivance, a convenient coincidence, or, in the final analysis, an uncritical and self-conscious accommodation to the surrounding culture. Not at all. It actually arose from their specific doctrine of God as the one who speaks and as such is bound up with their doctrine of God and not in any sense formally separable from it.

The point can be brought out clearly by looking at the Reformation understanding of the marks of the true church. Both Luther and Calvin argued for two such marks as essential: the Word correctly preached and the sacraments truly administered. What is significant is the practical priority which both give to the Word preached: for both Luther and Calvin, the true administration of the sacraments requires that this take place in the context of the Word, and that not a word hidden in a strange tongue, such as the Latin of the medieval mass, but spoken clearly in a manner which all can understand. This is the direct result of their understanding of God as a God who promises; and faith as something which grasps that promise. The whole idea of a promise carries with it certain ideas which must be true if the promise is to achieve its purpose: the person promising must be able to deliver on the promise, and therefore that person must be a 'known quantity' – they must have revealed themselves in words and actions to be the person which the promise, if it is to be valid, requires them to be; and the recipient must be able to understand it and act accordingly. Above all, a promise must have a verbal component: the signs of the sacraments cannot be trusted in and of themselves because, on their own, they have no intrinsic or stable meaning. They are, in themselves, only signs, and, for the Reformers, it is only in the linguistic context of the promise that they become, in a literal sense, significant and that what they signify can be grasped by faith. The aesthetic aspects of the Lord's Supper – the eating, the drinking, the visual imagery – were all important to the Reformers, but they were only important to the extent that what was said in the preaching and the words of institution created a context within which they could be understood. This is clear, for example, in the following comments by Luther and Calvin. First, Luther:

> What we deplore, in the servitude of the church, is that the priests take every care nowadays lest any of the laity hear these words of Christ.... [T]he whole virtue of the mass consisted in the words of Christ, when He gave testimony to the remission of the sins of all who believed that His body had been given for them and His blood shed for them. On this account, nothing is more important for those who hear mass than to meditate on his words carefully, and in fullness of faith. Unless they do that, all else they do is in vain.[7]

And then Calvin:

> [T]he right administering of the Sacrament cannot stand apart from the Word. For whatever benefit may come to us from the Supper requires the Word: whether we are to be confirmed in faith, or exercised in confession, or aroused to duty, there is need of preaching. Therefore, nothing more preposterous could happen in the Supper than for it to be turned into a silent action, as has happened under the pope's tyranny.... [L]et us understand that these words [of consecration] are living preaching which edifies its hearers, penetrates into their very minds, impresses itself upon their hearts and settles there, and reveals its effectiveness in the fulfilment of what it promises.... If the promises are recited and the mystery declared, so that they who are about to receive it may receive it with benefit, there is no reason to doubt that this is a true consecration.[8]

---

7. John Dillenberger, ed., *Martin Luther*, (Anchor Books: New York, 1961), 276, 278. The passage is taken from Luther's famous 1520 treatise, *On the Bablyonian Captivity of the Church*, from the section in which he attacks the contemporary church for undermining the promise-faith nature of Christian theology and practice by both conducting the mass in Latin and whispering the words of institution so that no-one could either understand or even hear what was being said.

8. John Calvin, *The Institutes of the Christian Religion*, ed. Ford Lewis Battles (Philadelphia: Westminster Press, 1960), 4.17.39.

In both cases the message is precisely the same: the benefits of the Lord's Supper are not available simply via the aesthetic experience of being present and partaking of the elements; the *words* of institution, the words of promise, need to be heard by the congregation and grasped by faith if the ordinance is to have its intended effect. The kind of salvation which the Christian God offers demands words, whether of promise or command, in order to define and delimit the nature of his relationship with his creatures.

Not surprisingly, this word emphasis which we find, for example, in Calvin's view of the sacraments, is reflected in the Reformer's understanding of the inspiration of the scriptures which is rooted not in the first instance in the subjective impact of those scriptures upon the reader but in the nature of scriptural authorship. As Calvin says in commenting upon the famous passage of 2 Timothy 3:16:

> In order to uphold the authority of the Scripture, he declares that it is *divinely inspired*; for, if it be so, it is beyond all controversy that men ought to receive it with reverence. This is a principle which distinguishes our religion from all others, that we know that God hath spoken to us, and are fully convinced that the prophets did not speak at their own suggestion, but that, being organs of the Holy Spirit, they only uttered what they had been commissioned from heaven to declare.[9]

Indeed, here we see two aspects of Calvin's Reformation theology which stand in stark contrast to current cultural and intellectual trends: an emphasis upon the central importance of words as the fundamental means of communication; and an emphasis upon the author and authorial intent rather than individual or community-centred reader response as determinative of a text's meaning.[10] God is a God who speaks, who communicates

---

9. John Calvin, *Commentaries on the Pastoral Epistles*, trans. William Pringle (Grand Rapids: Eerdmans, 1948), 248-49.

10. I am acutely aware of the issues of authorial intention, particularly with reference to a document such as the Bible where orthodox Christianity

himself and achieves that which he wishes to achieve in large part through the use of words: commands, promises, revelations of his power, grace, justice, and glory are made by words, or in a manner which can be expressed and communicated through the medium of words, a fact to which the very existence of the Bible and the centrality of the verbal declaration of God's way of salvation are, quite literally, eloquent testimonies.

Of course, the Reformation emphasis upon the centrality of words to salvation also finds expression in the manner in which individuals appropriate salvation for themselves. The fallenness of human nature and the overarching sovereignty and freedom of God mean that words in themselves have no power to convert or to achieve the purpose which God intended. Instead, words are combined with the activity of God's Spirit within a trinitarian economy of salvation which stresses the supernatural nature of God's grace. Again, we can turn to Calvin for a description of this. Continuing his comment on 2 Timothy 3:16, he remarks:

> The same Spirit, therefore, who made Moses and the prophets certain of their calling, now also testifies to our hearts, that he has employed them as his servants to instruct us. Accordingly, we need not wonder if there are many who doubt as to the Author of the Scripture; for, although the majesty of God is displayed in it, yet none but those who have been enlightened by the Holy Spirit have eyes to perceive what ought, indeed, to have been visible to all and yet is visible to the elect alone.[11]

---

stresses the reality and significance of both the ultimate divine authorship and the immediate human authorship of the various writers of the scriptural books. In this context, I find Kevin Vanhoozer's distinction between the intentional contexts of the various human authors and of the overall canonical purpose of God to be a useful one in doing justice to the riches of the biblical text without reducing, say, Isaiah 53 to precisely those limits which Isaiah himself consciously intended when proclaiming that passage: see Kevin J. Vanhoozer, *Is There a Meaning in This Text? The Bible, the reader and the morality of literary knowledge* (Leicester: Apollos, 1998), esp. 265.

11. John Calvin, *Commentaries*, 249.

The testimony of the Spirit, therefore, is what gives the words of scripture convicting power, convincing hearts and minds that it is no purely human fiction but a word from the living God. The same kind of pneumatic dynamism with respect to words is expressed by William Tyndale in an early passage when he is discussing the relationship between words, preaching, and conversion:

> When Christ is...preached, and the promises rehearsed...then the hearts of them which are elect and chosen begin to wax soft and to melt at the bounteous mercy of God and the kindness showed of Christ. For when the evangelion is preached, the spirit of God entereth into them which God hath ordained and appointed unto eternal life, and openeth their inward eyes, and worketh belief in them.[12]

The work of the Spirit is again of central importance, as this provides the words preached with their power. This is no culturally conditioned relationship but a profound theological connection which is rooted in an understanding of God as one who promises (and who, by definition, therefore speaks) and in an understanding of the biblical record which places great emphasis upon the creative and spiritual power of God's act of speaking to his creatures by his Spirit through his Word as expressed in words.

We can summarise this section, then, by making the following observations: the Reformation represented, in terms of theological culture, a move from a visual, aesthetic, and sacrament-centred theology to a word-based theology, where the written scriptures and the oral, preached word stood at the centre of belief and practice; this in itself, while reflecting a general movement in the wider culture towards words caused in no small measure by the advent of the printing press and the rise of literacy rates, was itself a theological development, linked to an understanding of God as a speaking, promising God whose

---

12. William Tyndale, *The First Printed English New Testament*, ed. T. Arber (London, 1871), 10-11.

spoken promises had to be grasped by the individual through faith. The centrality of words, spoken and written, was of the essence of the kind of salvation and Christian life which the Reformation proposed, and not merely an accommodation to the surrounding cultural milieu.

Knowing the Times

Having offered an interpretation of the biblical message and of Reformation theology centred on the theological status and function of words, we are now in a position to be able to evaluate the contemporary trends I outlined earlier in the chapter and offer a theological response.

To take the latter points, those about contemporary linguistic philosophy and 'postmodernism', the following observations suggest themselves. First, it is clear that the denial of any role to authorial intent in determining the meaning of a text is lethal to evangelical Christianity. If the meaning of texts is determined by what the individual reader or the reading community 'reads into' the said texts, then we are left with a God who simply cannot be known and even our best thoughts about him are no more than that which the German philosopher, Ludwig Feuerbach, accused all theological statements of being: nothing more than the psychological projection of our own religious and moral aspirations. Put simply, if the intent of the divine author does not inform and ultimately determine the meaning of scripture, then three things follow: scripture has no normative set or range of meanings; theology becomes merely reflection upon human religious psychology; and God remains an unknown, and unknowable, quantity. It is probably not going too far at this point to say that the deconstructive literary criticism which has been greeted with such incomprehensible glee by many Western academics in the eighties and nineties is simply the latest manifestation of human rebellion against God, of humanity's adamant refusal to give an account of itself before its Creator. It is nothing more than another attempt to silence God and thus to avoid our obligations to him. As Immanuel Kant and his followers thrust God into the realm of the noumenal, of those things that could not be known, and thus relegated him to the status of something one could only presuppose, but not know in any meaningful way, so deconstructionists, in killing off the author, relegate God to the status not simply of the unknowable but also of the unnecessary, and the radical epistemological chaos that has followed should be no surprise. Indeed, as Vanhoozer argues, the question of the author is at root the question of God, and denial of authorial intent is a profoundly theological move.[13] The death of God in the sixties has become the death of the author in the nineties.

Second, the suspicion with which words are viewed within much of postmodernism is also anathema to evangelical Christianity. If words and the interpretation of words are all about vying for power, about the manipulation of others, about control, then such a thing as God's promise of grace becomes not a promise of grace but a means of subtly subverting others and gaining control. Paul's declaration, for example, that we should be imitators of him as he is of Christ is transformed from a call to humility, self-denial, and the service of others, into a rather cynical, Uriah Heepish ploy to make others subservient to him. Yet the biblical text itself sees words as definitive of interpersonal relationships and invests much in the capacity of words to communicate, to establish relationships, and to evoke particular desired responses. Take Matthew 6:9-11: 'Which of you, if his son asks for bread will give him a stone? Or if he asks for a fish, will give him a snake? If you, then, though you are evil, know how to give good gifts to your children, how much more will your Father in heaven give good gifts to those who ask him?' The whole statement depends upon words being suitable vehicles for communication, and upon God being who he *says* he is. A radically deconstructive view of language would call into question both of these and completely transform the understanding and function of the passage. Christianity, then, should be inherently suspicious of such linguistic philosophies

---

13. '[T]he crisis in contemporary interpretation theory is actually a theological crisis,' Vanhoozer, 25.

and be very wary about flirting with them because they have profound and (from the perspective of orthodoxy) devastating theological implications. It is surely not without significance that the Fall was itself precipitated by the serpent indulging in the first apparent deconstructive reading of a text: by asking the lethal question 'Did God really say...?' he questioned both the reliability of God's words and the motivation (and thus the integrity) of the God who spoke them. The theological implica-tions of Genesis 3:1-5 would seem particularly important at the present time.

Third, as regards the cultural trend away from words to images, one could make a case for seeing this as, theologically, an undoing or a reversal of the Reformation and a reversion to aesthetic and sacrament-centred church life of a kind that defined much of medieval Catholicism. The general turn to the image and to the visual is not simply a phenomenon which of-fers the same cultural substance in a new cultural form. No – it is itself somewhat determinative of content. As the different reactions to the Kennedy-Nixon debate in 1960 demonstrated, radio and television, for example, do not offer two different ways of experiencing the same event, but actually two different events: in this case, radio offered a victorious Nixon, television a victorious Kennedy; but we need not restrict ourselves to the past – listen to a play on the radio and then watch the same on television or at the theatre; what you will have experienced is not two examples of the same work of art, but two entirely dif-ferent artistic phenomena. Thus, Marshall McLuhan's statement about the media, 'The medium is the message', would appear to be right on target and, when we recall the biblical emphasis upon words as central to the relationship between God and creatures, as picked up and re-emphasised in the Reformation, would also appear to have particular theological as well as more general sociological application. Given the significance ascribed by the Bible to speech in establishing and defining relationships, given the theological connection between the Word, hearing the Word, the work of the Holy Spirit, and the response of faith, and given the centrality of the pulpit and the words of God for the Reformation project, any attempt to marginalise or reduce the importance of words today must be seen as a theological act and not as a straightforward and value-neutral accommodation to current criteria of successful communication. The Reformation rediscovery of the gospel – of the Word of God – was intimately connected with the Reformers' rediscovery of the centrality of scripture and of preaching – of the words of God – and it is important that we understand the profound connection which exists between these two.[14]

A Challenge and an Opportunity?

As I conclude, I want to raise one important objection to what I have argued above: in arguing for a word/words-based theology in a culture which has become centred around the visual, is there not a danger of making Christianity an elitist movement which can speak only to the bookish, to the intellectuals, and to those comfortable with a word-based culture? This is a serious point and one which must not be dismissed out of hand: Christianity is explicitly *not* a religion biased towards the elite – intellectual, cultural or otherwise – and indeed, much in the New Testament would seem to indicate that, if anything, it will tend to be the exact opposite. We must, therefore, oppose with every fibre of our being anything which would turn the church into a club for the select intellectual few, and take care that we do not allow anything to contaminate our theology or church practice which would lead to any such elitism. Nevertheless, a number of observations can be made in defence of my position.

First, everyone still needs and uses words. One can be illiterate, but one must nevertheless speak and listen to others to form even the most rudimentary relationships or to operate

---

14. In this context, Dutch theologian J. Douma has some interesting observations to make with reference to the theological relationship between the verbal and the visual in terms of the Second Commandment: see J. Douma, *The Ten Commandments: Manual for the Christian Life*, translated Nelson Kloosterman (Phillipsburg: Presbyterian and Reformed, 1996), 35-72.

within society in any effectual manner. One can lack the power of speech or of hearing and yet one must still use words or their functional equivalents to enter into any kind of meaningful social intercourse. We may live in a culture where image is king, but words are still essential for us on the grounds of our status as social beings, and the implicit biblical teaching on language, from the creation story onwards, indicates quite clearly the necessity of language for relationships and communication. Whatever the trendy evangelical gurus tell me about the fact that Generation X does not respond to word-based messages, when I (or any other member of Generation X) go to the bank for a loan, the manager does not mime or dance before me; he or she explains in words what the nature of our relationship is; and, if I do not initially understand, it is his or her job to initiate me into the rules of the linguistic game that is being played. Certainly, if I default on my loan, claims that I belong to a post-literary culture will not cut much ice with the legal establishment. Furthermore, even within the culture itself there are signs that words enjoy considerable currency even at the recreational level: the popularity of bookshops (after pornography – surely the ultimate image as reality reductionism – book retailers are one of the biggest industries on the internet) indicates that even the written word has found a successful niche within a culture dominated by the television. Thus, the fact that our culture is now dominated in many areas by the visual does not mean that words are irrelevant or that something for which words are essential is by definition incomprehensible. That the surrounding culture is hostile to such a word-based movement as evangelical Christianity makes the task of communication that much harder from a human perspective, but it does not render it impossible.

Second, and more important, the power of the gospel is ultimately rooted in theological considerations, not sociological theory. It is not words on their own that move men and women to respond in faith to the promise of God, but the Holy Spirit himself, working in and through those words, who creates the positive response. In his dealings with the Corinthians, Paul makes it clear that, if his gospel were to be judged on the basis of his outward appearance (the visual) or even his rhetoric, then he would lose out to the super-apostles (1 Cor. 10–11). The gospel message simply did not depend on such superficial considerations for its success: it was rather the relationship of the foolishness of preaching to the foolishness of the cross, of the crucified Christ, and the power of the Spirit which gave Paul's words their power (1 Cor. 1:18–25; 2:4–5). In terms of priorities, therefore, we should make a thorough knowledge of Christ crucified and fervent prayer for the Spirit of God our priorities in meeting the current challenge posed by contemporary culture; after all, the content of the gospel has always been regarded as foolishness by the wider culture, and its success has never ultimately depended on assimilating its method of presentation to the norms of contemporary communication theory.

There are, then, good theological reasons for maintaining the centrality of words in the proclamation of God's Word. This is not to preclude reflection on what form that centrality might take in different contexts such as Sunday services, evangelistic outreach, Bible studies etc. Paul himself in the Book of Acts uses a variety of approaches in preaching the gospel and dealing with objections to his message, and such flexibility must be reflected in our own practice. Word-centred Christianity is not the same as a rigid adherence to the hymn-sermon sandwich style of service – after all, not all sermons use words to their best advantage in the current climate: we should be constantly reflecting on the world around us to see whether contemporary culture, in addition to the many hard challenges with which it faces us, offers any new and interesting opportunities for the gospel. For example, one aspect of televisual culture which the church would do well to heed – and to turn to its own advantage – derives from the pervasive impact of such things as soap operas: the way it has created a society of individuals who think in terms of stories. For the soap addict, the story is what creates reality, why characters in *Coronation Street* arouse such passions, why hundreds of thousands of people thought they knew Princess

Diana: they know the relevant stories, they have been taken into these fantasy worlds by the television, and their whole way of thinking about issues is shaped by the various story-lines and narratives which are pumped into their lives on a daily basis by the box in the corner. What an opportunity for the church! Is it not wonderful that God himself has provided us with the greatest story of all to tell? How does one tell someone who has never even heard of God who God is? Tell them the story, the most beautiful story ever told. Start at Genesis and work forward. The identities of Abraham, of Moses, of David, and of Christ and God himself are established by the biblical narrative; and that type of narrative framework comports well with the way in which contemporary Western men and women, boys and girls, soaked in televisual culture, think. We do not have to sideline words, even on human criteria, to communicate the gospel; we simply have to observe the basic narrative structure of the Bible itself, and the example of most of the great evangelistic sermons and 'outreach moments' in the Book of Acts, to realise that the narrative structure of the Bible is wonderfully suited to communicating the Bible's message in today's televisual society. We can tailor our preaching to suit this aspect of the modern world without compromising the Bible's message – indeed, we might find ourselves as a result being more faithful to it.

Cultural shifts have always presented great challenges to the church, and will certainly continue to do so. The church must always tread a difficult path: on the one hand, avoiding compromise with the world, on the other, being sensitive to the world around, not creating unbiblical barriers which hinder the work of the gospel, and being prepared to use different approaches and strategies in different situations. But we have to be clear, particularly at the present time, that words must remain central. Nearly twenty years ago, Carl Henry made the following statement, which was both an observation and, perhaps, a warning:

Multitudes in other civilizations and cultures of the past have listened responsively to mandarins and mullahs, swamis and gurus, and there is no reason to think that our technological mass media civilization will turn deaf to the importance and influence of words. If it hears no witness to the truth of revelation it is not because the blighting angel of technology has struck it dumb but because indifference in the Christian community allows the words of life to fade from sight and sound.[15]

Henry saw the centrality of words to human society, and the centrality of words to the message of the gospel: if the world ceases hearing those words, it is thus more than likely the fault of the church whom God has mandated to speak his words of judgment and grace to a fallen humanity. The Bible makes it crystal clear that words have a singular importance in relationships and communication, and have a singular theological importance in Christian salvation, an importance which was picked up and emphasised during the Reformation. As the great Scottish theologian, P. T. Forsyth, said at the beginning of one of the most important treatises on preaching ever written:

> It is, perhaps, an overbold beginning, but I will venture to say that with its preaching Christianity stands or falls.... Wherever the Bible has the primacy which is given to it in Protestantism, there preaching is the most distinctive feature of worship.[16]

Put simply, then, the question of the importance of words to the Christian church is a question of theology, not methodology: to marginalise preaching in our church life and outreach is to marginalise words; and to marginalise words will inevitably involve marginalising the Word himself.

---

15. Carl Henry, *God, Revelation and Authority*, III, 401.

16. P. T. Forsyth, *Positive Preaching and the Modern Mind* (New York: Hodder and Stoughton, 1907), 3.

THREE

THEOLOGY AND THE CHURCH: DIVORCE OR REMARRIAGE?

Introduction

The subject of this lecture, the nature of the relationship between theology and the life of the church, is of crucial importance at the current time and is highly appropriate for a lectureship established in honour of John Wenham who, in his day and generation, was one of the key figures in attempting both to make the academy more church oriented and the church more theologically informed. Such a task is a perennial one, for the simple reason that the breakdown of the theology-church relationship, like the breakdown of a marriage, is never straightforward nor is it simply a matter of technique. At heart, the fact that the issue impinges directly upon the relationship between God and his creatures means that it is a problem with a profound moral dimension. Thus, we need today to apply ourselves to healing the breach with as much vigour as those who undertook the task in previous years; and we must also be aware that the solution is not simply a question of bringing to bear the right technical skills on the problem but also of examining our hearts and minds in the light of what God has told us in his Word, and done in the person of Jesus Christ.

My lecture will be divided into three basic parts: in part one, I will offer a brief analysis of how the breach between theology and church manifests itself; in part two, I will offer four theses for the academy, not as an exhaustive program of reform, but as a suggested starting point or basic framework for pursuing reform; finally, in part three, I will offer four theses for the church which will aim to do a similar thing for our ecclesiastical bodies.

This was originally given as the John Wenham Memorial Lecture at a meeting of the Tyndale Fellowship Associates in 2002.

Grounds for Divorce

While the grounds for divorce between academy and church are no doubt complex, I will restrict myself today to a brief outline of the three issues which I suspect are most fundamental. These are the opposition of knowledge and experience; the differing presuppositions of church and academy; and the differing agendas of the two.

Regarding the opposition of knowledge and experience, this perhaps manifests itself most commonly in comments such as 'Well, so-and-so may know about God, but does he know God?,' and 'Professors at universities and seminaries may have lots of fancy words, but I just have plain and simple faith in Jesus Christ.' This is not just the kind of thought we find among Christians in the pews: Martyn Lloyd-Jones gave eloquent expression to precisely this kind of thinking in his disparagement of theologians such as Charles Hodge whom he dismissed as having no interest in revival.[1] It is, of course, a small step from dividing knowledge and experience in this way to setting them in fundamental opposition to each other. Evidence that this is the case can be found in the myriad of doctrinally vacuous hymns and choruses which form the heart of much evangelical worship today, where the message often seems to be 'Never mind the doctrine, give me the experience!' This, in turn, has the potential for the creation of what is basically a form of gnosticism, where the claims of the Christian are rendered invulnerable to criticism from outside by the fact that the one holding the beliefs has had a certain experience. Evangelicalism, with its stress on the necessity of the new birth and upon the cognitive effects of the Fall, is fertile soil for such gnosticism if the balance of biblical teaching on the relationship of knowledge and experience is lost.

On the other side, however, academic theology has often pursued a path which reduces the importance of experience to a minimum and makes everything a matter of technique – whether

---

1. See D. M. Lloyd-Jones, *The Puritans: their Origins and Successors* (Edinburgh: Banner of Truth, 1987), 7-8.

philosophical, grammatical, exegetical or whatever. This feeds straight through to the second point, the role of presuppositions. The academy, particularly as that academy has its agenda set by the secular university, can make no space for faith claims.[2] Thus, the epistemological importance of faith has been eliminated with the result that the church can ask with some justification exactly what it is about, say, Christian biblical scholarship which makes it Christian. Is it simply that, all things being equal after the application of standard academic techniques, the Christian will opt for the conclusion which most comports with orthodoxy? Or does the Christian biblical scholar's stance as a Christian affect the way that he or she approaches the biblical text at the outset? If the church has a problem in overstating the importance of Christian experience, the academy arguably has a problem in the way it tends to operate on a level playing field, where the connection between Christian commitments and attitude to the biblical text are not always apparent to those outside the scholarly community.

Finally, the agendas of church and academy are so often poles apart. The church sees the conversion to Christ of those outside as its primary reason for existence. This in turn leads to a certain impatience with complexities of doctrinal formulation, which can be perceived as obstructing or obscuring the basic simplicity of the message and the task. The academy, meanwhile, has its own agendas in a world which just keeps on getting more complex as, under the spiraling weight of information, disciplines become more and more fragmented and less and less connected

---

2. I am aware, of course, of the grand claims being made for postmodernism as opening up the university to faith perspectives. In my opinion, Christianity's claim to offer a grand narrative of universal significance, which, to maintain its own integrity, needs to deny the validity of the alternatives, will not win it any friends even in the postmodern academy. In fact, nearly a decade of teaching in British secular universities has convinced me that the major issue in university education is not postmodern epistemology but the alliance of free market policies, the interests of big business and an overarching pragmatism, a combination which serves more than anything else to restrict the kinds of research and discussion which take place.

to each other. The old medieval and Reformation idea that theology pursued at the highest academic level was to terminate in a unified academic discipline focused upon the needs of the church is simply untenable in the current climate: the highly technical diversity of the academy is simply unsuited to giving students a unified theological and ecclesiastical vision.

This, then, is the briefest of summaries of the basic grounds for the current divorce. I wish now to move to more positive proposals for overcoming this situation.

Four Theses for the Academy

1. The academy must reform its vision of God
The first thing that the Christian academy must do is reform its vision of God. Only when academics realize that the God with whom they deal is the awesome creator, holy and righteous, yet also infinitely tender and merciful, will they start to approach their calling with the necessary fear and trembling that it requires. God is not the object of theological study, in the way that a laboratory rat is the object of biological study – something to control, to dissect, to observe and analyze in a disinterested way; on the contrary, he is the subject of theological study, the one whose revelation of himself and whose gracious act of salvation in Christ make theology possible. In him we all live, move and have our being. Thus, all theological study must be conducted in conscious acknowledgement of and dependence upon God. Theologians are personally involved in and dependent upon him whom they study. That must shape our work at every level.

2. The academy must acknowledge the authority of scripture
Acknowledgement of the authority of scripture is surely basic to any theological work which claims the name of Christian and offers itself as in anyway useful to the Christian church. To say this is not to circumvent the complex problems that surround issues of canon, interpretation and hermeneutics, but it is to say that the Bible, as the Word of God, is unique in its relationship to God and in its function in the church, and that this must shape

the methodological and material status it is given by Christian academics. To treat the Bible as any other piece of literature is a profoundly theological move because to do so involves an implicit denial of the Bible's own claims to theological significance. This is not to say that there is not much to be learned from textual, cultural and linguistic studies but it is to say that the application of these various approaches to the biblical text needs to take into account the fact that the uniqueness of the Bible requires that such applications are not used to relativize the Bible's message. There is something presuppositional at work here: as Christians, the assumption that the one God speaks through the one Bible is taken as basic, and this provides a basic hermeneutical framework for biblical interpretation. Thus, for example, the Bible's theological diversity can never be emphasized to the point where its basic theological unity, grounded in its divine origin and its central subject matter, is undermined. The Christian presupposes a basic theological unity which provides the framework for interpreting each verse within the context of the whole. Without the basic assumption of theological unity rooted in the relationship between God and scripture, one is left with no basis for theological coherence other than the particular preferences of the reader.

The collapse in biblical authority is quite clearly evident in the academic world around us, where systematic theology, as classically understood as a study of the doctrines of God, creation, redemption etc. has all but disappeared, to be replaced on the university curriculum with courses such as 'Theology and hermeneutics,' 'Theology and Gender,' and 'Theology and Politics.' Each of these courses is no doubt worthy in its own way, but the real theological significance of any of these individual concerns can surely only emerge when they are set within the context of classic systematic theology as a whole, whose big picture then sets the agenda and brings these specific issues under the searching eye of a larger theological narrative. After all, can one understand gender issues without first coming to grips with God, creation, the Fall and the work of Christ?

Or take hermeneutics as an example: can one really engage in understanding language and scripture without first coming to grips with issues of the speaking God, revelation, sin, Christ and the work of the Holy Spirit? This could be a vicious circle, of course: we cannot interpret the Bible without a grasp of who God is; we cannot know who God is until we have interpreted the Bible. But dare I suggest that understanding the basic message of the Bible is perhaps not as complicated as many scholars seek to make it. I shall have more to say about the abuse of the doctrine of scripture's perspicuity in the church a little later, but I would like to make the point here that, while there are many things difficult to understand (and we have Peter's own words as our authority for that), the central gospel message of the speaking God is pretty straightforward. Scholars can tend to over-complicate things – partly because they of all people know that many things need to be nuanced – but this should not allow us to lose the basic simplicity of the gospel. After all, Christ points out that if even wicked earthly fathers, when asked by their children for bread will not give them a stone, then how much more will God give the Holy Spirit to those who ask. Surely he is here pointing not just to the great goodness of God but also to the basic perspicuity of language which exists in certain relational contexts such as that between father and child – even when allowing for the existence of moral depravity. From this, he clearly points towards the close relationship between that perspicuity of language and the meaningfulness of God.

When scholars start once again to take these things on board, acknowledging Scripture's authority, and accepting the basic clarity of its central message, they will, of course, be doing in the realm of epistemology precisely what I have said they must do in the realm of ontology: acknowledging God as sovereign and humanity as dependent upon him. God is, in a sense, the word he speaks, and we cannot take either side of this equation seriously without doing the same to the other half.

3. The academy must acknowledge the effect of sin upon scholars

If taking God seriously will inevitably involve taking scripture seriously and vice versa, it will also involve scholars once again re-examining human nature – the human nature in which they themselves participate – with a view to seeing how this impacts upon their work. One tendency in the academy which perhaps does more harm than we generally care to acknowledge is the effect of sin upon scholars themselves. This problem has been nicely put by Mark Thompson:

> All too frequently in modern theology fallibility is attributed to the biblical text as a matter of empirical certainty while at the same time the theological constructs of the writer are presented without the slightest hesitation or acknowledgment of provisionality. The impression is given that only in the current generation have the practitioners of theology been able to escape the impact of the fall upon the human mind.[3]

If much modern philosophy from Marx, Nietzsche and Freud onwards has exposed the ways in which hidden agendas serve to manipulate the way we think and act, surely as Christians, committed to an understanding of humanity, even redeemed humanity, as flawed and sinful, we too should take seriously the need for self-criticism in our approach to all of life. This includes scholarly work, where we should subject ourselves to constant self-criticism and be acutely aware of the fact that it is not just, or even primarily, the authors of the texts before us who are in the game of manipulation and deception.

4. The academy needs to return to traditional trajectories of theology

One of the grounds for divorce which I mentioned earlier was the differing agendas between church and academy. It would be easy at this point to say that the answer is simply that the academy needs to adopt the church's agenda but I would sug-

---

3. Mark Thompson, 'The missionary apostle and modern systematic affirm-ation,' in *The Gospel to the Nations: Perspectives on Paul's Mission*, edited by Peter Bolt and Mark Thompson (Leicester: Apollos, 2000), 378.

gest that that would not necessarily be a good thing, involving as it does the assumption that the church's agenda is itself in no need of correction. One of the obvious problems with this is that the church itself often seems to have great difficulty in defining its current agenda, for reasons which I will touch upon later. I would suggest at this point that a way to draw church and academy agendas back together is to return to the kind of theological trajectories along which theology in pulpit and academy was developed in the pre-modern era. These trajectories are to be found reflected in the great creeds and confessions of the faith. The Apostles' Creed, the Nicene Creed, the Athanasian Creed, the Belgic Confession, the Thirty-Nine Articles, the Westminster Confession of Faith, the Lutheran Book of Concord – all of these documents represent the fusion of pastoral and theological reflection upon the faith. Moreover, the questions they address, the identity of Christ, the nature of salvation, the definition of the church etc., are all vital and perennial questions; and the creeds and confessions pursue these questions in a manner which is both ecclesiastical and intellectually rigorous.

Ironically, evangelicalism, for all its pride in its orthodoxy, has seldom spent a great deal of time reflecting upon the creedal and confessional heritage of the church, and its scholarly representatives have proved no exception to this general rule, preferring the modern penchant for novelty over any notion that the church may indeed have got certain things basically right over the last two millennia. A little theological humility might serve us well here.

If these are four theses for the academy, how about the church? What should she be doing to help overcome the rupture with the academy?

Four Theses for the Church

1. The Church must rethink her emphasis upon experience
This is a tricky one, for the simple reason that evangelical Christianity, at least in its best form, is committed to the idea of the centrality both of doctrine (something which can be given

expression using a public vocabulary) and of the experience of God's grace in the life of the individual. The two things are formally separable and this, of course, means that the public distinctives of evangelicalism can be learned by those who lack the second, while the second can be claimed with no real grasp of the first. This has led, in some quarters, to a fear not simply that the truth might be preached through the mouths of those who are actually unbelievers but also that there can be a fundamental opposition between the two, the head and the heart, and that the latter, the heart, should therefore be given precedence. Now, I want to be careful here, in that I do not want to be misinterpreted as saying that conversion is not a prerequisite for ministry. It most certainly is; but I do want to say that the content and the efficacy of the gospel does not depend in any way whatsoever upon the moral qualities or salvific status of the individual who brings the message. The early church debated precisely this issue in relation to the efficacy of ministry of those who had fallen away during times of persecution and then returned to their old jobs when the persecution died down. It was decided then – and rightly so – that the Word of God was the Word of God, and not dependent upon the person bringing it to the church. To take any other position is surely disastrous, as none of us can know for certain what the state of anyone else's heart is; it is only because the gospel concerns the promise of God revealed in Christ that we can have confidence in the efficacy of the message preached. To put it more bluntly: it is better to have the gospel competently preached by one who proves to be an unrepentant adulterer than to have it preached incompetently by one who has been born again, precisely because it is the Word which is efficacious not the heart of the preacher.

This is perhaps putting it somewhat crudely, but it makes the point that the gospel is a message with content and not simply a case of one person communicating an experience to a group of others. That is, after all, the essence of old-fashioned liberalism – Christianity is the feeling, not the doctrine, and theology is simply reflection upon religious psychology not upon the revelation of God.

This has ramifications for various aspects of church life, not least in the realm of attitude towards learning. How many times have you heard the comment, 'Old Mrs Jones has walked with the Lord for fifty years and knows more of God than any professor with a PhD.' On one level, the comment might well be true – walking with the Lord in faith will get you into heaven in a way that mere possession of a PhD certainly will not. Nevertheless, when we grasp that the gospel is first of all a message, a proclamation of what God has done in Jesus Christ, and that experience comes as a response to that message, it is quite clear that a professor with a PhD may well have certain insights into that gospel message which Mrs Jones, for all her practical godliness, does not. Much of the anti-intellectualism which pours from pulpits in churches, from Reformed to charismatic, is the result of precisely this confusion between gospel as message and the believer's response in experience – a confusion which has just enough appearance of truth to be superficially plausible while resting on a fundamentally skewed understanding of what the gospel actually is. Only when the church comes to acknowledge in both belief and practice that the gospel is a message, not a feeling or an experience, will such fuzzy thinking (and much else) finally be put to rest. Indeed, this brings me to my second thesis for the church:

2. The Church needs to revise her worship practices in the light of the above.

Following on from the realization that the gospel is an announce-ment, not an experience, the church next needs to revise her response to that announcement. This I see as striking home in various areas. Most obvious, we need to reassert the centrality of the sermon as a part of worship, standing in positive relation to the songs sung and the prayers offered. If the gospel is an announcement of news, then guess what? It needs to be announced and pressed upon the gathered congregation, and that announce-ment itself needs to be understood as part of the worship of the church. Only as the gospel is declared can believers respond to it in the appropriate manner. Without this objective dimension, singing of songs becomes little more than the working-up of raw and somewhat contentless emotion. After all, worship is not just the songs that are sung; it is the word that is heard, to which the songs should be an appropriate response. This has numerous implications. For example, if your church is one where you cannot tell what the exact relationship is between what is said on a Sunday and what is sung on a Sunday, then you have serious problems that typical worship-war debates about contemporary versus traditional styles and frameworks will not even begin to address. In addition, if your preacher spends more time talking about himself, or the latest cultural trends, or making more applications than he does in straightforward exposition of the text, then these are signs that the confusion of gospel and experience might well be infiltrating your worship and thus your whole vision of Christianity.

None of this should be read as an attack on Christain experience. It is simply to point out that such experience is the result of the gospel, not the content of the gospel. To claim otherwise is to open the door to relativism. Once the gospel starts being presented primarily as that which brings such-and-such benefits, be they freedom from alcohol abuse or just emotional highs every once in a while, the distinctive particularity of Christianity is lost. Islam too gives people self-respect, cleans up neighbourhoods, gives a sense of purpose; self-help programs have brought many back from the brink of self-destruction to decent lives; and, while Christianity gives me a sense of meaning and worth, so, I believe, does ferret-breeding for some people. So what have I to say to the perfectly content ferret breeder? Not a lot, if Christianity is primarily about feelings, whether of satisfaction, happiness or otherwise. I have Jesus; they breed ferrets. Result in both cases: happiness. So what's the difference? The difference, of course, lies not in the experienced effect but in the cosmic bottom-line: Christ is God acting to save for all eternity; ferrets are good only as temporary distractions from the deeper realities and concerns of life.

To reinforce this message, we need to think carefully about our church services. The Presbyterian tradition to which I be-

long looks back to the great documents produced in the 1640s
as giving a good summary of what a Christian worship service
should contain: the reading and the hearing of the scriptures;
the preaching of the word; prayer (confession, adoration,
intercession); singing (in the case of the Westminster Assem-
bly, specifically of inspired materials – but that debate is for
another day); and the administration of the Lord's Supper and
baptism. Not a bad summary, and one which focuses attention
on the church service as held together by the content of God's
word, read, heard, and preached, to which prayer and singing
are a response. Anything else is surely Schleiermacherian – an
attempt to make human psychology and human experience the
basis of worship. This will ultimately prevent the church from
speaking across cultures. When worship discussions focus on
experience and style, then we are likely to deify the way we do
things and make it into some absolute by which all others must
be judged. That is simply wrong, and makes matters indifferent
(style and form) into something of the essence of worship. Let's
focus on the simple, straightforward *message* of reconciliation in
Christ, not our own experiences of church or whatever, as the
core of our church worship, and allow that to find expression
within the culture in which we find ourselves. Thus, when the
church gathers to worship, let her think about what passages
of scripture are to be read and heard, what is to be said in the
sermon, and what is to be sung; and let us make sure that the
content of each of these elements stands in an obvious relationship to the content of others.

Now, while none of this directly addresses the repair of the
relationship between the church and her friends in the academy,
it surely goes some way towards bringing the church back to a
correct understanding of the place of experience in Christianity,
and that in itself will prevent precisely the kind of anti-intellectual crusades which are predicated on the idea that deep,
theological knowledge can only impede spiritual progress. It
will also, I believe, reassure those church members who have
dedicated their lives to the pursuit of the study of theology at

the highest level that what they do is not necessarily trumped by the old lady who has walked with the Lord for fifty years. Both types of person make significant contributions; it is not an either/or, but surely a both/and.

Just as a final point in this section: this should also direct the church away from an obsession with revival and conversion as the main agenda behind our church services. Now, do not misunderstand me here. I am not saying that we do not want conversions; emphatically, we do. What I am saying, however, is that the Sunday service of the church is primarily for the equip- ping of the saints for the work of being a Christian Monday to Saturday. The church should be like a mother, nurturing us in our faith, giving us rest from the world and a tiny anticipation of what the fellowship in heaven will be like. On a practical level, given that few unbelievers bother coming to church these days, an evangelistic strategy based primarily upon Sunday services is, humanly speaking, not a strong one anyway. For all its faults with regard to content, the Alpha Course, I believe, has picked up on this problem and made significant contributions regarding the way forward for contemporary outreach. Sunday services should be focused more on equipping the saints. Of course, if an outsider attends our service, he should be made welcome, and should be able to understand what is going on and being said – one might add, he should be able to see an obvious connection between what is read, said, prayed and sung; but accommodat- ing him should not be the decisive priority in the service. In fact, coming into the presence of God's people worshipping a holy God should be an unsettling experience for the unbeliever. If you do not believe me, read and reflect upon the implications of 1 Corinthians 14:24-25.

3. The Church needs to acknowledge the role of tradition.

We've all met them, the no-creed-but-the-Bible guys and gals. What they usually mean is, of course, that, while they have a creed (even if it is 'no creed'), they cannot be bothered to write it down and want to privilege their view of the Bible (the right

one) over your view of the Bible (the wrong one). This is a difficult area, but I want to provoke you to think about this just a
little with the following comments.

First, there is a sense in which all evangelicals have no creed
but the Bible, in that we acknowledge only one ultimate epistemological source and criterion for judging statements about
God: the Bible. Given this, the statement is perhaps not so much
incorrect as misleading. It would be better to say 'No definitive
theological source but the Bible.' Nevertheless, in this sense I am
happy to be a 'no creed but the Bible' man.

Second, there is a sense in which we all depend upon extra-
scriptural creeds for our theology. As soon as we use the word
'Trinity', for example, we are using conceptual vocabulary which
is not found in the Bible but which has been developed and defined by the church over time. Now, I would immediately want
to argue that the language represents what scripture teaches. But
then, as soon as I claim that, I am doing no more than what the
church has traditionally regarded the creeds as doing: offering
a summary of, or a conceptual vocabulary for understanding,
simply what the Bible teaches.

Why then the modern fear of creeds? Well, this is of course part
of the wider cultural disposition of modern Western society and
is, interestingly enough, one of the key points of contact between
the academic world and the evangelical world. While scholars,
liberal and conservative, have developed a highly sophisticated
biblicism which routinely discounts the thoughts and insights
of the church over the centuries into the meaning of the biblical
text, so evangelicalism has developed a crude and unsophisticated
biblicism which routinely rejects (or, more often, simply ignores
as irrelevant) the history of church and theology.

So what are the advantages that the creeds give us? Well,
first, they remind us that the Bible is not its own interpretation.
It is not simply what the Bible *says* that is crucial but also what
it *means*, and the only effective way to give public expression to
that meaning is by the use of extra-biblical vocabulary and concepts. After all, there is not a heretic in the history of the church
who has not claimed to be simply believing what the Bible says,

or who has not quoted biblical texts by the score to justify his position. When meaning is at stake, it is not enough simply to quote Bible verses; the overall theological context of those verses is also necessary, as is the deployment of extra-biblical vocabulary. Of course, I firmly believe in the sufficiency and perspicuity of scripture, so I am not saying here that the Bible, on its own, is *meaningless*; rather, I am saying that it must be *interpreted*, but interpreted *on its own terms*. This act of interpretation necessarily involves the employment of language which is not found in the Bible and concepts which do not simply drop off its pages into our laps but which have to be carefully formulated in the light of the whole of scripture's teaching. As soon as we use extra-biblical language, as soon as we draw out the meaning of a passage, as soon as we explore the conditions which must hold true if a certain event is to have saving significance – as soon as we do any of these things, we move ourselves into territory which is, in one sense, 'extra-biblical.' This is where the creeds come in: they are simply summaries of biblical teaching, using language and concepts which have been publicly endorsed by the church as orthodox throughout the centuries, thus providing an orthodox scheme and vocabulary for theological life. And this is where my second point about creeds becomes significant.

Second, creeds place us and our times in perspective. God's Word contains precious promises about how he will lead his church into all truth. Now, we know from the history of the church and from the current diversity among the Christian body that any notion of an automatic, quasi-mechanical relationship between God, God's truth and the public theological pronouncements of the institution of the church is simply untenable. All such statements coming from whichever church need to be scrutinized by scripture to see if they are biblically coherent. There is a sense, however, in which the pendulum has swung too far in the direction of an automatic hermeneutic of suspicion regarding historic theological creeds and tradition. Nowadays, it is more likely to be assumed that the church has generally got it wrong than that she has got anything right. I commented to colleagues just recently in reference to the views on justification

and Christology being put forward by a leading British New
Testament scholar that I was left wondering if this person,
who identifies himself as orthodox, thought the church had
managed to get anything right regarding the Bible over the last
1900 years. The attitude of the Reformers was very different:
they rejected those traditions which were explicitly rooted in an
understanding of the church as having new, revelatory powers
after the closing of the canon, but they took very seriously the
exegetical, theological and, above all, the creedal tradition of
the church and only modified or, as a very last resort, rejected
it at those points where scripture really did make it untenable.
The difference is one of attitude and culture, I think: they oper-
ated with a basic hermeneutic of trust, albeit biblically critical
trust; too often today we operate with a basic hermeneutic of
suspicion, perhaps for the most part uncritical suspicion. Yet,
if we take the church seriously and if we take God's promises
to the church seriously, such knee-jerk iconoclasm can only be
a bad thing.

I might go further and say that the church needs more than
a hermeneutic of trust towards the creedal and confessional
trajectories of the past. There is also a need for a hermeneutic of
humility. As with the immature arrogance of those scholars who
feel that their PhD on some few verses here or there in the Bible
qualifies them to redefine orthodoxy *tout court*, so the church of
today also needs to learn humility in relation to the past. When
some creedal formula or doctrinal position has been held by the
church with vigour for some considerable time, then the church
of today should think very carefully before deciding to change
it in any fundamental way. Our perspective is so limited; our
moment in time so insignificant in the grand scheme of things;
therefore, we do well to see the church's creeds, confessions
and traditions as giving us some perspective by which we may
relativise ourselves, our contribution, and our moment in history. I have lost count of the number of times I have heard church
leaders declare that 'the church needs to move beyond....' (add
your own central tenet of the faith: the cross, the wrath of God,
sin, the Trinity, justification by faith, the authority of scripture

– I've heard them all cited). Underlying such sentiments are not so much a hopeless naivety but rather a tragic arrogance, an arrogance which implicitly says that the church in the past did not really get the gospel and that only in the present day have we approximated some kind of doctrinal maturity. I would suggest that reflection upon the creeds and confessions of the church might well go someway to overcoming the chronological arrogance (to use C. S. Lewis's phrase) that afflicts the church as it should also do in the academy.

As a postscript to this section – for both church and academy – I mention a challenge I like to issue in class to students who are tempted to disparage the Nicene Creed: given that this creed has served the church well for over a thousand years, one should be very careful before one abandons it; but if after reflection, one can come up with a formula which will deal with biblical material as effectively, will enjoy such wide acceptance in the church, and which will do the job just as well for the next thousand years, one should not be afraid to propose a new formulation. Strange to tell, I have yet to have any takers for that one.

4. The Church needs to realize that not all answers to questions about the Bible are that simple.

If rejection of the witness of history and tradition is something the academy and the church both have in common, then the thing over which they most dramatically differ has to be the complexity or otherwise of the Bible. As noted above, the tendency in academic circles is to stress the ineradicable complexity of all biblical questions, a tendency fuelled by the fragmentation of the discipline as a whole and by the kinds of literary-critical approaches which take a peculiar delight in scepticism about the stability of textual meaning. In the church, however, the idea that there are any complicated questions is often not countenanced at all. Even though Peter himself tells us that Paul wrote many things that are hard to understand, the idea that interpreting the Bible competently takes skill and training is alien to much of the evangelical world. I well remember giving a lecture on how the Puritans of the seventeenth

century established high standards for ministerial education
at a British seminary. At the end of my talk, I was challenged
by one individual who saw what I said as running counter to
what he took to be the basic thrust of Paul's pastoral letters,
of the nature of saving faith, and of scriptural perspicuity. Of
course, he read the relevant quotation from a translation of the
Bible, implicitly conceding that none of these things made void
the need for somebody, somewhere to have a good grasp of the
vocabulary, grammar, syntax and historical context of koine
Greek. The certainty of faith and the perspicuity of scripture
were never intended to mean that all answers to everything
were simple, any more than the idea of scriptural sufficiency was
intended to mean that the Bible gives answers to all questions
about life, such as what time the next bus arrives. Rather, they
pointed to the fact that the Bible's basic message was clear and
easy to grasp by even the simplest of minds, a point to which
the Reformers and Puritans held while at precisely the same
time pursuing theological education and study at the highest
level. The church needs to understand this once more. She has
always faced complicated questions; once, these focused on the
doctrine of God; now, perhaps, they focus on the relationship
of one culture to another, of how the church in the West, with
all of her financial and educational resources, can both learn
from and serve the church in the South and the East, with her
massive numbers, her signs of great blessing from God, but her
economic and intellectual dependence upon the North and the
West. These are tough areas which demand careful and humble
reflection and which cannot be resolved by simplistic claims to
truth on one side or the other, claims which are, of course, more
often claims to power than to truth.

    These then are my brief theses for academy and church. I am
probably naïve in thinking that this lecture will make any difference; but if it helps just one person to start thinking about
these issues, whether in agreement or disagreement with what
I say, I think I will have gone some way to fulfilling the kind of
mandate which the John Wenham Lecture carries with it.

FOUR

THE PRINCETON TRAJECTORY ON SCRIPTURE: A CLARIFICATION AND A PROPOSAL

Introduction

It is, I believe, still true that most evangelical doctrines of scripture take the tradition of old Princeton Seminary, prior to the
collapse of orthodoxy there in the 1930s, as the starting point for
reflection. This is the case both for those who wish to develop
their own understanding of scripture in continuity with that of
Hodge and company, such as Roger Nicole, and those who wish
to break with the tradition in significant ways, such as Donald
Bloesch. Like Augustine on grace for Western theologians, so
Princeton on scripture for evangelicals is a basic part of any
dogmatic discussion.

Over recent years, however, it seems to me that much of what
passes for evangelical comment on the Princetonian trajectory
is to a large degree inaccurate and ill-informed. Frequently, the
only citations of primary sources (if any) one can find in such
discussions bear an uncanny and suggestive resemblance to the
footnotes of Jim Packer's 'Fundamentalism' and the Word of God; and
thus the association of old Princeton, and particularly Warfield,
with all manner of positions, particularly on scripture, persists,
probably because too few are prepared to stand up and question
how much first-hand knowledge undergirds the numerous brash
statements of the critics.

A glance at any of the various compendia of Warfield's writings which are available – supremely, the ten-volume Oxford
University Press edition recently reissued by Baker Book House
– should immediately alert us to the fact that we are probably
not dealing with a theological dunce. The knowledge of church
history and biblical exegesis, and first-hand acquaintance with
contemporary theology, particularly that of Dutch Calvinism
and German liberalism, reveals Warfield as a man far more

competent in the broad sweep of the theological discipline in his day than the fragmentary nature of the contemporary theological scene will allow any of us to be today. We should take him seriously, then, if for no other reason than that he was a learned and thoughtful individual who neither adopted nor abandoned theological positions without first thinking through such a move very carefully indeed.[1]

The Context of Warfield's Theology

When we turn to Warfield's theology proper, we must ask first what kind of theology it is. It is no good focusing simply on a few isolated passages in the various writings on scripture: the doctrine of scripture itself stands within a complex of other doctrines; and the approach Warfield uses to this doctrine will be determined by a variety of factors, both in terms of the immediate issues and opponents to which he is addressing himself, and in terms of the tradition of theological reflection within which he himself stands. Theology is a traditionary action and must always be understood as such.

To take the latter first, Warfield, like his other colleagues at Princeton Theological Seminary prior to 1929, was the latest in a long line of representatives of Reformed Orthodoxy. This was a theological tradition which found its roots in the Reformation of the sixteenth century and in the formal development of Reformation theology by Protestants in the universities in the years subsequent to that momentous event. It was catholic, in that it attempted to stand in line with the great creeds of the early church and also sought to interact with the various contours of

---

1. The breadth of Warfield's knowledge and expertise can be grasped by looking at the bibliographical list of his publications (minus those he wrote on cattle breeding!) assembled by John E. Meeter and Roger Nicole in *A Bibliography of Benjamin Breckinridge Warfield 1851-1921* (Phillipsburg: Presbyterian and Reformed, 1974). Useful collections of his writings are the ten-volume set from Baker Book House, the five volumes edited by Samuel Craig and published by Presbyterian and Reformed between 1948 and 1958; and the two-volume *Selected Shorter Writings*, edited by John E. Meeter (Phillipsburg: Presbyterian and Reformed, 2001).

the contemporary theological scene; Reformed in that it took its cue from the Reformed wing of Protestantism, with the various theological distinctives which that implied; and confessional, in that it looked to a body of confessional material, supremely in Princeton's case, the Westminster Standards; and articulate, since one of the legacies of Reformed Orthodoxy was that it gave men like Warfield a vocabulary and a set of concepts with which to give precise formulation to their theological thoughts. Like their predecessors in the seventeenth century, Princeton professors sought to study theology at the highest level and were well acquainted with the thought and literature of those whose beliefs they repudiated. Thus, Charles Hodge, the greatest systematician of Princeton, was trained at the best continental universities, was a good friend of the mediating theologian, Tholuck, and even includes a footnote in his *Systematic Theology* where he reminisces nostalgically about attending Schleier-macher's church while in Berlin, and of the great German's habit of singing hymns with his children around the fireside.[2] Then, as mentioned earlier, Warfield's own writings show a profound acquaintance with German liberalism and an appreciation, albeit critical, of the aims of various German theologians. Therefore, however much some (both foes and friends) now associate Hodge, Warfield and company with fundamentalist Reformed pietism and reactionary obscurantism, such was not actually the case.

Given this context, it is no surprise to find that the Princetonian understanding of scripture is embedded within a complex of theological doctrines that had been developed within Reformed theology from the sixteenth century. As with the thought of their predecessors, inspiration and infallibility/inerrancy do not function for the Princetonians as axioms from which all else is deduced; rather, the Princeton understanding of the nature of scripture is determined by its position in relation to a number of other points.

Most important of these is the nature of human knowledge of God. In the late sixteenth century, the Reformed theologian

---

2. Charles Hodge, *Systematic Theology*, 3 vols. (Grand Rapids: Eerdmans, 1993) 3.3.9, II, 440, n. 1.

Francis Junius introduced an important distinction into Reformed orthodoxy: that between archetypal and ectypal theology. The distinction, cribbed from the medieval philosopher John Duns Scotus, was used to divide divine self-knowledge, or archetypal theology, which is by definition perfect and infinite, from human knowledge of the divine, which is by definition limited and imperfect. The point is important to grasp, indicating as it does that there is a critical relationship between the two, such that God retains his hiddenness, sovereignty, and incomprehensibility even after revealing himself; yet gives humans knowledge of himself which, because it rests upon his own self-knowledge, is nonetheless true for all its limitations.

Hodge does not explicitly use the distinction, but clearly holds to its basic substance, as in the following quotation from his *Systematic Theology*:

> While, therefore, it is admitted not only that the infinite God is incomprehensible, and that our knowledge of Him is both partial and imperfect; that there is much in God which we do not know at all, and that what we do know, we know very imperfectly; nevertheless our knowledge, as far as it goes, is true knowledge. God really is what we believe Him to be, so far as our idea of Him is determined by the revelation which He has made of Himself in his works, in the constitution of our nature, in his word, and in the person of his Son.[3]

Thus, limited, partial, imperfect knowledge is yet true knowledge. This is a vitally important point to grasp because it serves to provide a basic context for the Princetonian understanding of scripture as the cognitive ground of theology and thus for the Princetonian understanding of scriptural authority and inspiration.

This distinction is closely related to the idea of accommodation, the notion that when God communicates with humanity he does so in a manner consistent with human capacities. Accommodation has a good pedigree in the Christian tradition, going

---

3. Charles Hodge, *Systematic Theology* 1.4.A, I, 338.

back at least as far as Augustine and deployed most famously by John Calvin. Warfield himself rarely refers to the concept of accommodation but it is there in his writings, and his thought seems entirely consistent with the tradition on this point.[4]

The reason I mention this is to put into perspective Hodge's famous reference at the start of his *magnum opus* to theology as a science and to the Bible as its book of 'facts'.[5] He is here using the language of the inductive scientist, to which his Princeton education, steeped as it was in Scottish Common Sense Realism, would have exposed him. Such language is a little unfortunate, allowing some scholars to impute to Hodge the view that the Bible contains nothing but a storehouse of facts of the 'Napoleon died on St Helena' or 'Two plus two equals four' variety; in other words, the Princeton tradition is seen as regarding the Bible as a book of information and data. Such arguments frequently cite the language of 'facts' as if this in itself was sufficient to win the point, and thus leave themselves open to the objection of committing the root fallacy. In fact – if you will pardon the pun – Hodge uses the language of facts to posit an analogy between theology and science in order to underline that, as the empirical world is the cognitive foundation for empirical science, so the Bible is the cognitive foundation for theology. The language is, from a modern/postmodern perspective, perhaps unfortunate, but the point is substantially the same as that which has been made by Christian theologians throughout history. This is made clear by Warfield himself in his classic 1896 essay on 'The Idea of Systematic Theology', where he argues that a science presupposes three things: the reality of the subject matter; the capacity of the human mind for knowing the subject matter; and a medium of communication whereby the subject matter

---

4. *The Inspiration and Authority of the Bible* (Philadelphia: Presbyterian and Reformed, 1948), 93. It is worth noting Tony Lane's criticism of Jack Rogers and Donald McKim on this point: see A. N. S. Lane, 'B. B. Warfield on the Humanity of Scripture', *Vox Evangelica* 16 (1986), 77-94.

5. *Systematic Theology*, Introduction 1.1, I, 1-2.

is brought to the mind.[6] He then proceeds to define theology
as a science:

> The affirmation that theology is a science presupposes the
> affirmation that God is, and that He has relation to His creatures....
> The affirmation that theology is a science presupposes the
> affirmation that man has a religious nature, that is, a nature capable
> of understanding not only that God is, but also, to some extent,
> what He is; not only that He stands in relations with his creatures
> but also what those relations are.... The affirmation that theology
> is a science presupposes the affirmation that there are media of
> communication by which God and divine things are brought before
> the minds of men, that they may perceive them and, in perceiving,
> understand them.[7]

Thus, scripture is the medium by which divine things are brought
to the mind of the believer. It is within this wider context that
not only must the language of science and facts be understood,
but also the Princeton elaboration of the nature of scriptural
authority must also be set. It is to this that we now turn.

Inspiration and Revelation

The nature of scripture for traditional, conservative, biblical
evangelicalism is often discussed in terms of the two concepts of
inspiration and revelation. W. G. T. Shedd, one of the great nine-
teenth-century American Presbyterian dogmaticians, has this to
say on these points in his three-volume *Dogmatic Theology*:

> Inspiration is like Revelation, in that it is a superhuman influence
> upon the particular person selected to be the organ of the Divine
> mind. But inspiration goes no further than to insure freedom
> from error in presenting that truth which has been obtained in
> the ordinary ways in which men obtain truth; while revelation
> discloses new truth that is inaccessible to the ordinary human
> mind. A man may be inspired, and yet not reveal anything. Much
> of the Bible is of this kind. But a man to whom a revelation is

---

6. B. B. Warfield, *Studies in Theology* (Edinburgh: Banner of Truth, 1988), 55.
7. *Studies in Theology*, 55-56.

communicated, is also inspired to express and record it. Inspiration is more of the nature of instruction and information.[8]

In other words, broadly speaking, inspiration refers to the mode of delivery of the scriptures, in a manner which guarantees freedom from error, while revelation refers to the content of the scriptures, in this case, truths which would not be available to natural reason or were not discovered by normal empirical means of investigation.

On inspiration, of course, the key text is the 1881 article of the same name by A. A. Hodge and B. B. Warfield in the *Presbyterian Review*.[9] The article fell into two parts: the first, by Hodge, dealt with the doctrinal foundations and definition of inspiration; the second, by Warfield, dealt with apparent discrepancies etc. in the scriptural text. There is, however, no reason to treat the contents of the whole as reflecting anything less than the views of both men.

Considering the subsequent reputation of the piece among liberal evangelicals as symbolising the epitome of conservative dogmatising about scripture, it is worth noting that the article originally stirred up considerable opposition from conservative elements among American Presbyterians as conceding too much to the left. The relevant documents can be found in the 1979 reissue of the piece by Roger Nicole, gathered in Appendices 1 and 2.[10] The controversy in part focused on the rejection by Hodge and Warfield of dictation as the literal mode of inspiration, preferred to argue for a providential concurrence between the divine and human authors as the means of establishing the scriptures as reliable and inspired. As the original article declared:

---

8. W. G. T. Shedd, *Dogmatic Theology*, 3 vols (Nashville: Nelson, 1980) I, 70-71.

9. 'Inspiration', *Presbyterian Review* 2 (1881), 225-60. This was reprinted, with an introduction by Roger R. Nicole as a book, *Inspiration* (Grand Rapids: Baker, 1979). In preparing this paper I have used the pagination in the Nicole edition.

10. *Inspiration*, 73-82.

> We prefer to use [the term *inspiration*] in the single sense of God's
> continued work of superintendence, by which, his providential,
> gracious, and supernatural contributions having been presup-
> posed, he presided over the sacred writers in their entire work of
> writing, with the design and effect of rendering that writing an
> errorless record of the matters he designed them to communicate,
> and hence constituting the entire volume in all its parts the word
> of God to us.[11]

This is followed by an assertion that inspiration is both plenary
(i.e. coextensive with the biblical canon) and verbal (i.e. extends
to the very words themselves). In this latter context, Hodge
and Warfield are emphatic in their rejection of a mechanical or
dictational view of inspiration:

> This view [of dictation]...we repudiate as earnestly as any of
> those who object to the language in question. At the present time
> the advocates of the strictest doctrine of inspiration in insisting
> that it is verbal do not mean that in any way the thoughts were
> inspired by means of the words, but simply that the divine su-
> perintendence, which we call inspiration, extended to the verbal
> expression of the thoughts of the sacred writers, as well as to the
> thoughts themselves, and that hence the Bible, considered as a
> record, an utterance in words of a divine revelation, is the word
> of God to us.[12]

In this assertion, Hodge and Warfield offer a view of inspiration
which comports with their view of human agency as a whole:
in the Reformed tradition, human action and divine will are so
dovetailed that neither is negated or swallowed up by the other.
Both are operative in every historical action. There is, to use
Warfield's terms, a concursus, a running together, of the divine
and human which preserves both the reality and integrity of
both.[13] What is different in the context of scripture is that the

---

11. *Inspiration*, 18.
12. *Inspiration*, 19.
13. E.g. *The Inspiration and Authority of the Bible*, 94-96; also see the discussion in Lane, 84-85.

divine superintendence of the writing of the scriptural record is specifically and explicitly concerned with the accurate recording of the subject matter of revelation. This parallel between inspiration and providence is worth noting if only because one of the schools of left-evangelicalism, that of Clark Pinnock, has rejected the classic doctrine of inspiration in part on precisely these grounds, seeing perhaps more clearly than some orthodox Arminian evangelicals how closely tied are the two doctrines.

As an aside, we should acknowledge that Warfield later nuanced his understanding of revelation to allow for three different modes: theophany or outward manifestation; internal suggestion; and concursive operation. In the first two categories, he does indeed make room for words being given directly by God to his chosen human mouthpiece – but this is the result of the demands of the scriptural text or history where, as in the case of Moses, God met with the prophet and told him exactly what words to write down.[14]

All of these arguments serve to underline Warfield's basic contention that what scripture says, God says. This is why he feels able to characterise the scriptures as *oracular*. Indeed, in his article 'The Church Doctrine of Inspiration', he says the following:

> [The church] looks upon the Bible as an oracular book, – as the Word of God in such a sense that whatever it says God says, – not a book, then, in which one may, by searching, find some word of God, but a book which may be frankly appealed to at any point with the assurance that whatever it may be found to say, that is the Word of God.[15]

The language of oracle therefore is used by Warfield to contrast the orthodox view of scripture with liberal, Romantic or mystical notions which turn the scriptures from the Word of God into human reflections upon God. This point is worth noting carefully, because at least one evangelical critic of Warfield has

---

14. *The Inspiration and Authority of the Bible*, 83-96.
15. *The Inspiration and Authority of the Bible*, 106.

used Warfield's language of oracle and its cognates to ridicule his position on scripture.

In a paper delivered to the Tyndale Fellowship in 1995, the distinguished Anglican theologian Anthony Thiselton drove a wedge between on the one hand Warfield and his followers, who, he argued, tended to view the authority of scripture as residing in its status as the conveyor of true information, and on the other those in the tradition of James Orr and G. C. Berkouwer, who tended to root its authority in its salvific function. Between these two poles, Thiselton presents his own view, drawing on speech-act theory, as offering a constructive path through the middle.[16]

There are a number of points at which that paper is vulnerable to criticism, not least the author's determination to present the Warfield position as pretty well exclusively informational, yet to do so on the extremely narrow evidential base of just a handful of select and isolated quotations from the Princetonian's writings. In addition, Warfield is explicitly misrepresented in terms of his use of the incarnational analogy in describing the relation of the divine and human in scripture,[17] and various assertions are made without any supporting evidence, as if the truth of highly debatable assertions is so well known as to be above dispute. For example, we are told that

> those who associated themselves with Warfield's view fell increasingly under the spell of regarding revelation primarily under the single model of information.[18]

---

16. Anthony C. Thiselton, 'Authority and Hermeneutics: Some Proposals for a More Creative Agenda,' in Philip E. Satterthwaite and David F. Wright (eds), *A Pathway into the Holy Scripture* (Grand Rapids: Eerdmans, 1994), 107-41.

17. Compare Thiselton's comments on pages 125-26 with the pages which he himself cites in Warfield, *The Inspiration and Authority of the Bible*, 162-63, where Warfield injects precisely the notes of caution *re* distinguishing scripture from incarnation which Thiselton himself counsels.

18. 'Authority and Hermeneutics', 110.

No evidence is cited to support this view; and the fact that some modern defenders of biblical infallibility or inerrancy may have fallen into this error scarcely allows us to damn the whole tradition or the Princetonians to whom it may look for its authority. At best this is a *post hoc, propter hoc* argument; at worst it is simply playing to a sympathetic audience who will always tend to assume that scholarly emperors would never parade naked in public.[19]

I mention these points not to undermine Professor Thiselton's significant contributions to thinking about scripture and interpretation but merely to indicate how careful we must be when reading the opinions of even the most learned and generally reliable theological scholars on the issue of the Princeton approach to biblical authority. It is surely only fair that Warfield is exegeted carefully with due respect to his context and his overall theological positions, and then judged on his own merits and those of the best of his followers rather than by the rash statements of some zealous but perhaps inferior disciple.

What Thiselton has done, in fact, is to miss the point of the language of inspiration and oracle in Warfield's writings. For Warfield, authority does not ultimately lie merely in the informational content of scripture; it lies in the fact that scripture is what God wanted it to be. It uses the words, the language, the grammar and syntax which God intended, and it does this because it is divinely inspired, oracular, that what it says, God says, and that what it does, God does. This approach does not necessarily involve the reduction of the content or purpose of scripture to the primary model of information, or the transmission of information, as we shall see shortly when we come to discuss his notion of revelation. If, perchance, some chose to abuse it in that way, it is not the fault of the doctrine of inspiration as Warfield articulated it in and of itself. Some people use

---

19. And, of course, Harold Lindsell's book, *The Battle for the Bible* makes its totemic appearance as a means of making the inerrancy position ridiculous by association: see 'Authority and Hermeneutics', 113-14, where this is presented as the logical extension of the Warfield 'informational' approach to biblical authority.

hammers to do damage rather than hang up pictures; it does not mean that the person who designed the hammer can be held responsible for any acts of vandalism to which his hammers may be applied; and if the Warfield approach has been used to do damage, that is the fault of particular practitioners, not of Warfield himself.

The information-function dichotomy is not a new criticism with Thiselton. It was also pushed very hard in the book by Jack Rogers and Donald McKim, *The Authority and Interpretation of the Bible* (San Francisco: Harper and Row, 1979), which sought to legitimise the functional approach of Berkouwer by providing it with a suitable historical pedigree. While Thiselton's article is to an extent dependent upon their work for his historical understanding (though not for the force of his dogmatic proposals), it has to be said that this particular book has been so decisively demolished by scholars such as John Woodbridge, Richard Gaffin and Richard Muller that its primary usefulness today lies in its status as a classic example of the political trajectories surrounding debates on scripture in American Presbyterianism in the 1960s and 1970s. Warfield, like his Dutch contemporaries, Abraham Kuyper and Herman Bavinck, refused to separate scripture's formal nature from its material content: both were intimately connected, with the form being determined by the content or intention, whether that be the communication of historical information, the interpretation of God's great saving acts, or the many kinds of speech-acts (to use the modern jargon) which God performs by scripture. One suspects that the gap between Professors Warfield and Thiselton is not as great, nor the modern contribution as earth-shattering, as the latter might like to believe.

Having looked at inspiration, we must now glance briefly at Warfield's understanding of revelation. Warfield's thought in this area is summed up in his 1915 article, 'The Biblical Idea of Revelation,' which was written for the *International Standard Bible Encyclopedia*, edited by James Orr. Warfield's understanding of the basic structure of revelation, as divided into general/

natural revelation and special revelation sets him firmly within the historic Reformed tradition. Special revelation, unlike general/natural, is saving: it reveals God as the God of covenant, of Christ, and of salvation by grace. As such, it possesses a certain historical structure of which Warfield is well aware, being a biblical scholar and sensitive to the shape of redemptive history expounded in the Bible:

> In contrast with His general, natural revelation, in which all men by virtue of their very nature share, this special, supernatural revelation was granted at first only to individuals, then progressively to a family, a tribe, a nation, a race, until, when the fulness of time was come, it was made the possession of the whole world.[20]

Revelation for Warfield thus follows the historical flow of God's electing love as recorded in the scripture, culminating in Christ and thence moving out to embrace the whole world. Warfield was, of course, both a colleague and a good friend of Geerhardus Vos, the pioneer of conservative biblical theology along the redemptive-historical path later picked up and developed by Herman Ridderbos, Willem Van Gemeren etc. In addition, the contribution of covenant theology to Reformed thought over the centuries ensured that Warfield was working against a theological background in which the movement of God's salvific work in history was a central theme.

This has an important impact upon his understanding of revelation: it is emphatically not reduced to scripture but in fact encompasses God's saving acts in history, which scripture then serves as both the epistemological foundation and the interpretation. I quote Warfield at length on this point:

> Revelation is, of course, often made through the instrumentality of deeds; and the series of His great redemptive acts by which He saves the world constitutes the preeminent revelation of the grace of God – so far as these redemptive acts are open to observation and are perceived in their significance. But revelation, after all, is

---

20. *The Inspiration and Authority of the Bible*, 79.

the correlate of understanding, and has as its proximate end just
the production of knowledge, though not, of course, knowledge
for its own sake, but for the sake of salvation.... Nor can this
particular series of acts be thought to have as its main design the
production of knowledge; its main design is rather to save man.
No doubt the production of knowledge of the divine grace is one
of the means by which this main design of the redemptive acts of
God is attained. But this only renders it the more necessary that
the proximate result of producing knowledge should not fail; and
it is doubtless for this reason that the series of redemptive acts of
God has not been left to explain itself, but the explanatory word
has been added to it. Revelation thus appears, however, not as
the mere reflection of the redeeming acts of God in the minds of
men, but as a factor in the redeeming work of God, a component
part of the series of His redeeming acts, without which that series
would be incomplete and so far inoperative for its main end.... It
is, in one word, itself a redemptive act of God and by no means the
least important in the series of His redemptive acts.[21]

Two things flow from this understanding of revelation. First,
there is no need to regard the doctrine of inspiration as flatten-
ing scripture to the level where all parts are equally important.
Certainly, Warfield's doctrine demands that all parts are equally
authoritative in a formal manner, in that all parts are there just
as God wanted them to be: the details of the murder of Ehud as
well as the covenant promise made to Abraham. But materially,
it is the accounts of the great saving acts and their explanation
that hold centre stage. This is, of course, why Warfield did not
regard subscription to his understanding of inspiration as of
the essence of the Christian faith. It was, he felt, the most consistent and coherent position; but one could be a Christian and
hold to a more limited understanding of the Bible's authority.
Christianity, he boldly declared at one point, would be true even
without inspiration, or even without any Bible at all, because
the great saving deeds of God take place in history and would
have been witnessed to by real historical people who would

---

21. *The Inspiration and Authority of the Bible*, 80-81.

have provided reliable, if not infallible, accounts of what went on. Belief in inspiration is the capstone of Christian belief, not its foundation.[22] The church believes in inspiration because Christ and the apostles taught the doctrine and it is therefore an important part of consistent Christian faith, though not absolutely necessary in terms of salvation, a point Warfield himself never tires of making.

The second point is that scripture as a redemptive act, as providing the explanation of God's salvific acts in history, does not necessitate the reduction of its content to that of objective information, as others noted have claimed. It is true that it demands that revelation has a certain cognitive content, that it appeals to human understanding, that it partakes of a linguistic form; but it does not require that scriptural revelation be reduced to the level of the statement 'Two plus two equals four', which I assume (for he gives no precise definition) is what Professor Thiselton means when he speaks of the Warfield tradition being preoccupied with informational content. The statements of scripture, because they relate to God's saving actions in history, are in their very essence existential in terms of the demands they make upon the reader or listener.

To take a trivial analogy: when my tax return arrives each year, along with its notes of explanation, those notes make demands upon me. They contain much information, but if I simply read them, understand them at 'the informational level' and then move on to other more pressing matters without filling out the return, then one could argue that I had really misunderstood the notes – and that excuse will be of no use to me when the Inland Revenue descends upon me in six months time. The notes do not just tell me how the form should be filled out; in the context of the receipt of the form, they implicitly demand that I fill it out, or face the dire consequences, robbing me as they do of any excuse for failing in my duty. Likewise, to be told that my house is on fire involves a certain level of cognitive content; but to claim that to see the statement as involving cognition reduces it to the

---

22. *The Inspiration and Authority of the Bible*, 210-12; cf. 121-23; also *Inspiration*, 7-8.

level of mere information is misleading. It is similar when one comes to the scriptures. The information which they contain must be accurate if it is to be of any use; but this is intimately connected to God's great saving acts in history and therefore makes demands upon the whole person who reads or hears it. To force a distinction between information and function in the manner which has been imputed to Warfield is to miss entirely the basic relationship which he sees that scripture has to God's saving acts and, indeed, the status he ascribes to it as one of those saving acts.

Can We Use Warfield Today?

The most pressing question regarding Warfield's position on scripture is, of course, whether it is of use to us today. The debate on scripture, as Tony Thiselton indicates in his article, continues in evangelical circles to run along pro- and anti-Warfield lines; is this necessary, or even useful as a means of approaching the problem?

Obviously, in a paper such as this it is impossible to solve all the problems surrounding current evangelical debates on scripture, and so I will restrict myself to just three points which I hope will be of use to you as you seek to wrestle with these issues in your studies and your own Christian life.

The first point is a simple one: just because those who attack the Princeton tradition in general, and Warfield in particular, are world-renowned scholars who may be cleverer and better read than you or I, that does not necessarily make them correct. As with all academic books you read (and, indeed, any productions by members of the pro-Warfield camp such as myself), check the footnotes, check the sources, read the quotations in the original texts so as to determine the immediate theological context of particular statements. You will be surprised how often confident claims about this or that aspect of the Warfield tradition are based upon a less than sure-footed reading of the primary materials, a contrived and forced interpretation of a particular sentence, and sometimes upon no reading of primary material at all.

The second point concerns what one might call 'the third way' of approaching scripture, which is being proposed most notably by Tony Thiselton but also by Kevin Vanhoozer and Nicholas Wolterstorff (though all three have different emphases and differing degrees of sympathy with the tradition of Old Princeton). Certainly, I think anything which flags up the fact that scripture is more than a collection of facts is to be welcomed, and much of the speech-act analysis is extremely useful in understanding not just what God is *saying* in the Bible but also what he is *doing*. Nevertheless, I remain unconvinced regarding two of the implications of the work, particularly of Tony Thiselton, regarding the old Princeton approach.

First, I am not convinced that speech-act theory represents a particularly significant breakthrough in terms of its positive contribution to understanding the Bible. That the Bible contains a variety of literary genres, that God says and does different things through different parts of the Bible, seems to me to be something the best theologians have always appreciated. What speech-act theory does is provide a precise, if sometimes somewhat obscure, vocabulary by which this truth can be expressed and understood. Perhaps one might add that this conceptual vocabulary bears fruit in that it allows us to be more self-aware of what much of the church's exegetical tradition has done all along. To be fair to the speech-act lobby, scholars such as Tony Thiselton are well aware of this; but it is useful – and perhaps conducive to Christian modesty – to remind ourselves of this fact once in a while.

Second, I am not convinced that speech-act theory renders entirely redundant the kind of questions about inspiration which Warfield was asking and seeking to answer. The promise of salvation given to Abraham is intimately linked to God's saving acts in history and, from our point of view, intimately linked to the fact that Abraham was an historical person. The Bible contains historical narratives; while the literary forms of these narratives are undoubtedly of crucial theological significance, their literary form does not eliminate the fact that such narratives also make claims to historicity; and it binds God's mighty speech-acts of command and promise to particular mighty historical acts. It does matter to the Christian that God actually spoke these particular words of promise to Abraham; it does matter to the Christian that God actually raised Christ from the tomb on the third day; it does matter to the Christian that when Paul writes his letters, he got it right and did not get it wrong. Yes, words do things; but God's words are spoken by God, and backed up by God's deeds. One can abandon the Warfield position on scripture if one wishes, but one must then proceed to replace it with something which is adequate to the task of ensuring that the cognitive content of Christian faith (e.g. the knowledge that the God who promises is both willing and capable of delivering on his promise) is safe and secure. I myself do not see why the Warfield position is not totally adequate for, and compatible with, the kind of speech-act approach to scripture which some are proposing, providing that its adherents avoid the caricature of that position which flattens scripture to the level of objective information and nothing more.

My third point arises from the excellent essay by Tony Lane, 'B. B. Warfield on the Humanity of Scripture', the only piece of work of which I am aware which focuses on this aspect of Warfield's position. At the close of this article, the author makes an interesting proposal regarding the way forward for evangelical scholars who wish to stand in continuity with Warfield's insights yet who also wish to take the argument forward in a manner which is useful in the contemporary scene:

> The way forward is not to weaken Warfield's firm grasp of the divine authorship of scripture, any more than denial of the deity of Christ is the cure for docetism. What is needed is not a *lessening* of our grasp of scripture as God's word, but a *heightening* of our grasp of its human authorship. Warfield gave full *formal* acknowledgment to the humanity of scripture, but he can justly be accused of failure to develop the implications of it. The way to avoid a split between the dogmaticians and the biblical scholars

is not to abandon Warfield's view of scripture as God's word but to develop his doctrine of its human authorship.[23]

I find myself in formal agreement with this statement; given the fact, as Tony Lane acknowledges, that the polemical context of Warfield's work was one in which it was precisely the divine authorship of scripture which was at stake, he inevitably stressed that at the expense of the human, and it is here that work remains to be done.

I think, however, that I would still want to qualify the proposal in a modest way. It is true that, over recent years, Warfield's position has found a more comfortable home with the systematicians such as James Packer and Wayne Grudem than with the guild of evangelical biblical scholars, probably in large part because the latter are generally concerned in the first instance with the form of scripture which is, of course, ineradicably human. The systematicians have a duty, therefore, to indicate that the Warfield trajectory on scripture is perhaps broader, and in principle makes more allowances for the human dimension than its popular image might suggest. There is even in the famous Hodge-Warfield article on inspiration a certain amount of leeway left on the issue of date and authorship of particular books in the Bible, with the one proviso that no conclusion in this realm should contradict scripture's own testimony on the matter if it makes one.[24] In addition, regarding chronologies and numbers, the Hodge-Warfield distinction between accuracy and exactness would again seem to give room for manoeuvre on the part of biblical scholars.[25] Finally, as Tony Lane himself argues, despite Warfield's commitment to the idea of inerrant autographs, the whole framework of concursus and human authorship, not to mention statements in Warfield's own writings, would seem to leave sufficient space for making allowances for the editorial prehistory of particular definitive

23. Lane, 90.
24. *Inspiration*, 39.
25. *Inspiration*, 28-29.

texts.[26] It would be useful to remind biblical scholars of all of these things, lest they inadvertently throw the baby out with the bathwater.

Nonetheless, the battle within evangelicalism today is once more focused on the divine authorship of scripture. It is not, I would suggest, the humanity of scripture which is generally being neglected by the guild of evangelical biblical scholars. Thus, while evangelical systematicians may need to think out their position on human authorship more thoroughly, biblical scholars certainly need to be made to take account of divine authorship, and to do so sooner rather than later. The lack of critical reflection within evangelical biblical scholarship upon what the statement that scripture is God's Word actually means, what limits this places upon investigation, what implications it has for method, is a worrying sign. This is only exacerbated by the divorce that now exists between systematics and biblical studies and the paranoia in some circles that, whatever else one can do, one must not approach the text with any theological agenda – a position which is self-defeating as there is no approach to the biblical text which does not involve theological presuppositions of some kind.

The issue is not, I think, one where it is the raising our grasp of human authorship that is most pressing but of seeing precisely how the divine and human are compatible. Warfield had an answer in his doctrine of inspiration and his notion of concursus. He was not an idiot; he saw that this was one of the central problems of scripture which the Christian theologian or biblical scholar had ultimately to face; maybe his solution is imbalanced or not entirely adequate; but if that is the case, then we should aim to build on it, and to build better, rather than

---

26. Lane, 82, citing *The Inspiration and Authority of the Bible*, 156. Warfield is, as Lane notes, speaking about the prehistory of the text as the product of a single author, but there is no obvious reason why this idea cannot be expanded to include an editorial process involving several individuals providing, of course, that this does not contradict scripture's own statements about itself. For example, it would seem to me that, for the scholar committed to the supreme authority of scripture, Christ's statements about authorship trump all critical alternatives.

simply refuse to face up to the problem at all, to chop the text up any which way during the working week and then bow our heads in reverence before its teaching on a Sunday. If scripture is part of God's redemptive action in history on behalf of humanity, if what scripture says and does, God says and does, as Warfield claimed was the case, then these are not idle games which the scholars are playing; they have profound and serious implications; and we would do well to face up to the issues with the seriousness and intelligence of Warfield even if we should find that we cannot go with him all the way.

FIVE

THE GLORY OF CHRIST:
B. B. WARFIELD ON JESUS OF NAZARETH

Introduction

When B. B. Warfield died eighty years ago, in 1921, J. Gresham Machen, his Princeton colleague, commented that old Princeton had indeed passed away with him. It is arguable that this was not much of an exaggeration, such was the stature of a man whose scholarship had been recognised in the award of an honorary degree from the University of Utrecht, who had been on personal terms with such luminaries as Abraham Kuyper and Herman Bavinck, and whose writings, at both popular and academic levels, had influenced a generation of Christians in the church and in the academy. Yet, it is true to say that Warfield is little known today outside of the narrow confines of the evangelical world, that his piety is appreciated far more than his scholarship is understood, and that his wide-ranging theological contributions are not appreciated even by those for whom he symbolises theological orthodoxy. Indeed, when we ask the question, For what is Warfield known today?, we are likely to elicit responses which focus on his articulation of biblical inspiration and authority, his arguments for the cessation of the supernatural gifts of the Spirit, or his cautious arguments in favour of theistic evolution. Yet, as even a glance at the ten-volume selection of his writings that were published by Oxford University Press in the early part of the twentieth century reveals, his range was much broader than these three narrow foci would suggest.[1] For example, he also wrote on church history,

---

This chapter was originally given as the Evangelical Library (London) Lecture in 2001.

1. *The Works of B. B. Warfield* (Grand Rapids: Baker, 2000). This is a reprint of the ten-volume edition published by Oxford University Press.

producing essays on Tertullian, Augustine, and Calvin which still have merit today. He also engaged in extended study and refutation of perfectionism, providing the church with one of the most comprehensive historical and theological analyses of holiness teaching ever produced. In addition, he also found time to write reviews on many of the significant theological books of his time, continental as well as Anglo-American, revealing not only extensive linguistic competence but also a thorough and accurate understanding of the liberal positions that he rejected. Indeed, it is, I suspect, true to say that Warfield read his liberal opponents with more care, courtesy, and all-round theological learning than liberals have, over the years, applied to his work. To reduce Warfield's significance to a few doctrinal topics is thus to miss the real greatness of the man whose life was driven far more by a desire to restate the classic Reformed faith in an articulate and intelligent manner than simply to focus on one or two controversial points.[2] Indeed, his greatness is captured neatly in a recent comment from the pen of Mark Noll and David Livingstone:

> Even in the long line of outstanding conservative theologians from Old Princeton that stretched from Archibald Alexander...to J Gresham Machen...Warfield stands out. In that distinguished company, he was the most widely read, had the greatest skill in European languages, displayed the most patience in unpacking arguments, and wrote clearly on the widest range of subjects.[3]

Today, therefore, I want to break with the traditional canon of evangelical topics upon which Warfield is consulted and look instead at a handful of writings from his pen devoted to Christol-

---

2. Cf. the comment of Mark Noll and David Livingstone: '[A]lthough several of Warfield's positions continue to exert considerable influence among theological conservatives, the defence of Calvinism that loomed so large in his own work receives far less attention today.' 'Introduction' in B. B. Warfield, *Evolution, Science, and Scripture: Selected Writings*, edited by Mark A. Noll and David N. Livingstone (Grand Rapids: Baker, 2000), 19.

3. *Evolution, Science, and Scripture*, 17-18.

ogy, the person and work of Jesus Christ. In the words of John Murray, 'There is no subject on which Warfield's master mind showed its depth and comprehension better than on that of the person and work of Christ.'[4] And, we might ourselves add, there is no subject which stands more central to Christian orthodoxy than Christology. All great theologians have wrestled with the person and work of Christ, and the greatest theologians are those who have offered the most penetrating insights into precisely this area of doctrine. Thus, if we are to appreciate Warfield's contribution to the Christian church in all its fulness, we need to develop some comprehension of his work on Christ.

Before looking at Warfield's writings on Christ, it is, however, necessary to make one or two preliminary observations on the slightly peculiar nature of his scholarly output. As the husband of an invalid and housebound wife, Warfield did not enjoy quite the same freedom with regard to his career as is normal among academics. His domestic duties inevitably meant that, for much of his academic life, he neither travelled much beyond the borders of Princeton nor had the kind of uninterrupted research time necessary for the production of weighty tomes. Thus, the vast majority of his writings are what one might almost call occasional pieces – articles for journals and for encyclopaedias rather than sustained and lengthy monographs. This is not to belittle their learning nor their significance, nor, in some cases their length; but it is to indicate that the reader will look in vain in his books for the kind of classical, all-embracing doctrinal synthesis that is found, say, in that of his Princeton predecessor, Charles Hodge. Warfield addressed specific topics in a thorough fashion; he was not involved in the careful division and arrangement of topics that are demanded by the genre of a comprehensive systematic theology. The result is that the reader who is interested in Warfield's understanding of Christ is dependent upon the volumes of his works which gather together articles and sermons rather than upon any single systematic treatise.

---

4. John Murray, *Collected Writings*, 4 vols (Edinburgh: Banner of Truth, 1976-83), III, 359.

Given this fact, I shall today focus on just a small number of his Christological pieces, on the basis that the diversity of material on this subject in Warfield's writings makes it impossible to do justice to all facets of his work in this area. What I want to bring out is the fact that, for Warfield, Christ was glorious and Christology was a glorious subject upon which to reflect. This is simply because, for Warfield, Christ is God manifest in the flesh, the supreme revelation of God to humanity, and the supreme act of God's love towards a lost and dying world.

Warfield on Incarnation

It almost goes without saying, of course, that Warfield's Christology makes no attempt to break with the classic tradition of orthodoxy whose basic framework was established by the early church at the Councils of Nicea and Chalcedon. For him, Christ is both fully divine and fully human, consisting of these two natures, unmixed and uncorrupted, within the one person, Jesus of Nazareth. At the end of his article 'The Person of Christ according to the New Testament', he quotes the Chalcedonian definition in full, describing it as 'nothing...but a careful statement in systematic form of the pure teaching of the New Testament'.[5] Thus, Warfield places himself self-consciously within the tradition of the church which, in terms of explicit formulation, stretches back to the third century. He is, in the true sense of the word, a Catholic theologian.

Given modern theological misgivings about the language of substance and personhood as inadequate or inappropriate for discussing the identity of Christ, a number of comments are apposite at this point. It is, of course, a truism that the language of Chalcedon, of substance and personhood, is absent from the New Testament, and, of course, no advocate of the Chalcedonian definition denies this. Warfield's own view of the Chalcedonian definition is that it functions as a presupposition which makes

---

5. B. B. Warfield, *The Person and Work of Christ*, ed. Samuel G. Craig (Philadelphia: Presbyterian and Reformed, 1950), 37-70. The quotation is from page 70.

the teaching of the Bible comprehensible as a single, unified whole. To quote him on this point:

> Only on the assumption of this [the Chalcedonian] conception of Our Lord's person as underlying and determining their pres-entation, can unity be given to their representations; while, on this supposition, all their representations fall into their places as elements in one consistent whole.[6]

This is an important point which has a general application well beyond its specific concerns. For a start, it flags up Christ's humanity and divinity as the only means of making coherent sense of the Gospel accounts of his life. It is thus not in the first instance an exercise in metaphysical speculation but rather an attempt to think out the necessary presuppositions about his person which make sense of the historical account of his actions and teachings given in the Gospels. This is a very important point, particularly at a time when theological diversity is some-thing of a buzzword among biblical scholars. The current trend is, I am sure, intimately connected to the increasing subdiscipli-nary specialization of higher learning, fuelled in large part by the information revolution; but Warfield is surely correct to point to the presuppositional nature of our theological approach to the Bible. If we go to the Bible without a commitment to the unity of revelation and the coherence of the biblical witness at the level of epistemology, then we will inevitably find ourselves drawing certain conclusions from that, such as the God of the Old Testament is not that of the New or the way of salvation for Paul is not the same as for James. It is perhaps no surprise that the Chalcedonian definition is being called into question by theologians at exactly the same point in time as the funda-mental theological unity of the Bible is also being subjected to vigorous assault.

For Warfield, the idea that Christ is one person in two sub-stances is one of the necessary counterparts of his commit-ment to the unity of scripture's teaching: in other words, it must be

---

6. *Person and Work*, 58.

true because it allows the church to make sense of the Bible's teaching about Christ. The formula itself is not inspired in the way that the Bible is inspired; it is not therefore sacrosanct; one can indeed go to heaven without ever having heard of the definition; but it is nonetheless a necessary presupposition, implicit or otherwise, if the message of the Bible concerning Christ is to be properly and thoroughly understood.

Many will be aware, of course, that the twentieth century saw a sustained and vigorous war waged against the Chalcedonian definition by mainstream theologians. The critique of Chalcedon is nothing novel: it represented in its very formulation the triumph of one theological party over another; and it also gave rise to a series of further Christological questions which many theologians came to conclude were lethal for its viability as an expression of biblical teaching. These questions tended to focus on the alleged failure of the language of the two natures to do justice to the unity of the one person. To put it bluntly, the formula has been seen by many as woefully inadequate or highly problematic when dealing with issues such as the knowledge of Jesus Christ and of his earthly sufferings. Indeed, it is often alleged that the Chalcedonian formula actually generates difficulties with these issues which would not exist if the language of two natures–one person had never been adopted. The specific background of such criticism against which Warfield was working was that of the German liberal schools who, while diverse in many respects, were all working within the anti-metaphysical trajectory of theology after Kant. As such, their attacks on two-nature Christology stand in interesting continuity with those of an earlier anti-metaphysical movement within Protestantism, that of the Socinians of the seventeenth century. Both groups saw the definition as involving the infusion of Greek metaphysics and philosophy into theological discussion, and thus saw the rejection of traditional language about the incarnation as part and parcel of returning to a more pure, more truly biblical, theology. This was a point of which Warfield himself was clearly aware.[7]

Historically, of course, the Chalcedonian definition was formulated by the church in the context of needing to emphasise the unity of the Son with the Father in terms of divinity, while yet also establishing his unity with humanity in the Incarnation. To lose sight of Christ's unity with the Father would prevent Christ from being a revelation of the Father. Yet, the understanding of incarnation also had to be done in a manner which avoided a mixing of the divinity and the humanity. Such a mixing would have produced a Christ who was neither divine nor human in any real sense. Nor could the church define Christ in a way which would lead to a radical separation of the two natures, because this might have undermined the unity and thus the identity of Christ as the one mediator. As such, the final formula agreed upon at Chalcedon was considered to be a superb balancing act, which, while not satisfying everyone in the early church, was generally considered to have avoided both of the lethal pitfalls outlined above.

So important were the truths which this formula expressed to Warfield that he himself was to argue that the current crisis in theology and the church in his day was directly related to the various attacks on the Chalcedonian definition. Such attacks, he declared, were simply attacks on the doctrine of Incarnation itself and thus upon the very hinge of Christianity.[8] Its critics, of course, did not see it in quite the same way; they regarded the formula, or at least the way the formula had been generally understood and used, as being inadequate for the task for which it was intended, that of doing justice to the Bible's own account of Christ. Now, such attacks took various forms, but one consistent pattern of criticism, that the traditional understanding of the Incarnation prevents justice being done to the humanity of Christ, found its clearest expression in the varieties of so-called kenotic Christology which were prevalent in

---

7. Warfield himself explicitly addresses this in his article 'The "Two Natures" and Recent Christological Speculation' in *The Person and Work of Christ*, 211-62.

8. *The Person and Work of Christ*, p. 211.

the late nineteenth and early twentieth centuries, and against which Warfield argued with some vigour.

Warfield on Kenosis

The kenotic theory, or rather theories, of the Incarnation, with which Warfield had to do, had arisen in the nineteenth century both in the context of Reformed-Lutheran ecumenism, where it was seen as a means of overcoming the historic differences between the two traditions in the area of Christology, and also as a means of offering potential solutions to some of the questions raised by two-nature Christology. Kenoticism in its broadest outlines is summarised by Louis Berkhof as follows:

> [Kenosis] signalized the doctrine that the Logos at the incarnation was denuded of His transitive or of all His attributes, was reduced to a mere potentiality, and then, in union with the human nature, developed again into a divine-human person.[9]

In other words, the kenotic theory was the response of certain theologians to the problems raised by the biblical accounts of, for example, Christ's growth in knowledge, his apparent ignorance of certain things, and the general finitude of his earthly existence. While classic Reformed theology had traditionally overcome these issues by focusing on the way in which the communication of properties between the natures took place within the one person, kenoticists rooted the solution in the divestment by the divine nature of its divine properties upon the hypostatic union of the human and the divine within the Incarnation. There was variety among the advocates of kenotic Christology themselves, with some even going as far as to question the usefulness of incarnational language about Christ, given the radical nature of self-abasement to which the Son subjects himself. Names associated with kenotic theory include Thomasius, Delitzsch, Gore and, slightly later, Forsyth and Mackintosh.

---

9. Louis Berkhof, *Systematic Theology* (Edinburgh: Banner of Truth, 1958), 327.

Before looking at Warfield's response, we need to spend a moment or two reflecting upon the attractiveness of such theological proposals. On the surface, kenotic theory offers a solution to the very great mystery that surrounds how the infinite God can come and dwell with humanity. In short, he voluntarily divests himself of many of his divine attributes. This would appear to offer a convenient solution to some of the more complicated questions raised by the traditional understanding, such as why Christ appears to be ignorant of certain information, such as the timing of his second coming. In fact, of course, it merely solves one set of metaphysical questions at the expense of creating a whole new set of the same, such as, Is a God shorn of his attributes still meaningfully 'God' in any sense?

Second, kenotic theory seems to offer a way of underscoring important theological points such as the dramatic divine condescension which is involved in the mission of the Son, and the identification of God with men and women in their humanity. These are central biblical concerns, and kenoticists regarded their formulation as being far more capable of doing them justice than the traditional understanding. Nevertheless, advocates of orthodoxy would never have regarded their own position as undermining these emphases and would have argued that the kind of condescension and identity proposed by the kenoticists was ultimately not that proposed by the biblical texts.

This brings us to the third point: while the theological background to kenoticism is undoubtedly important, the doctrine claims its most significant support in the exegesis of Philippians 2:7. At the end of the day, the doctrine stands or falls by whether it makes sense of, or is demanded by, biblical teaching, and the key passage in this context is the passage in Philippians 2 which speaks so movingly of Christ's condescension in his mission to earth. It is here, therefore, that Warfield chooses to focus his arguments against the kenotic theory.

Warfield's refutation of such a position has two major pillars. First, he argues that the verb and tense in Philippians 2:6 referring to Christ 'being God' does not indicate a state of affairs that held true once and has now come to an end, but something which continues to be the case. Thus, the verse contains no hint of any movement from divinity to non-divinity in the act of Incarnation.[10] Indeed, Warfield neatly summarises this position as follows:

> So far is Paul from intimating, therefore, that Our Lord laid aside His Deity in entering upon His life on earth, that he rather asserts that He retained His Deity throughout His life on earth, and in the whole course of His humiliation, up to death itself, was consciously ever exercising self-abnegation, living a life which did not by nature belong to Him, which stood in fact in direct contradiction to the life which was naturally His.[11]

From this statement, he then moves on to discuss the key word in Philippians 2:7: *ekenōsen*. This is translated in the Revised Version as 'emptied himself', a rendering which clearly leaves open the very great possibility of a kenotic Christology. In the Incarnation, Christ can thus be seen to *empty* himself of his attributes of deity, the very point which kenotic Christology seeks to establish. Warfield, however, repudiates this as a mistranslation of the verb. He points to the four other occurrences of the verb in the New Testament, indicating that, in each case, the verb is not used in a literal or ontological sense but in the metaphorical sense of 'to make of no account' or 'to render void'. Thus, the verb here would seem to require a translation not so much of 'emptied himself' as 'made himself of no account'.[12] Warfield expresses this as follows:

> Paul, in a word, says here nothing more than that Our Lord, who did not look with greedy eyes upon His estate of equality with God, emptied Himself, if the language may be pardoned, of Himself; that is to say, in precise accordance with the exhortation for the enhancement of which His example is adduced, that He did

---

10. *The Person and Work of Christ*, 40-41.
11. *The Person and Work of Christ*, 41.
12. *The Person and Work of Christ*, 42.

not look on His own things.... He took the 'form of a servant,' and
so was 'made in the likeness of men.' But His doing this showed
that He did not set overweening store by His state of equality
with God, and did not account Himself the sufficient object of
all the efforts. He was not self-regarding: He had regard for others. Thus he becomes our supreme example of self-abnegating
conduct.[13]

For Warfield, then, the significance of the Philippians passage
lies not so much in what it says about the nature of Christ, as
in what it says about how we are to respond to Christ: in his
Incarnation, in the humiliation which he undergoes for us and for
our salvation, he is the supreme example of how we as Christians
are to see ourselves and our status in relation to others. In other
words, the passage has ethical considerations as its primary
concern; it is not in the first instance a statement about the
mechanics of the Incarnation with respect to the relationship
between the two natures.

It is perhaps important at this point to remind ourselves of
why the rejection of kenoticism in its various forms is important.
To the mind not schooled in the implications of certain theological controversies, Warfield's concern to reject the kenotic reading of Philippians 2:7 might seem like mere arguing over words.
In fact, nothing could be further from the truth. The kenotic
theory is dangerously vulnerable on a number of grounds. First,
as shown above, the exegetical basis for the notion is extremely
slim. Second, the idea that the second person of the Trinity can
divest himself of his attributes of deity in the Incarnation raises
the serious question of whether Jesus Christ of Nazareth can be
said to be fully God in any meaningful manner. To say that he is
fully God but that he has divested himself of his attributes would
seem to require an understanding of deity whereby being and
attributes are decisively separable. Warfield does not address
this issue in precisely these terms, but it is quite clear from his
understanding of the Incarnation as revelation that he is well

---

13. *The Person and Work of Christ*, 42-43.

aware of this kind of problem. Referring to the teaching of the
Letter to the Colossians, he declares the following:

> He who looks upon Jesus Christ sees, no doubt, a body and a man;
> but he sees the man clothed with the body, so he sees God Himself,
> in all the fulness of His Deity, clothed with the humanity. Jesus
> Christ is therefore God 'manifested in the flesh' (1 Tim. 3:16), and
> His appearance on earth is an 'epiphany' (2 Tim. 1:10).[14]

For Warfield, then, as for Christian theology in general, the
Incarnation is the manifestation, the revelation of God, in the
human flesh of Christ. The glory of Christ is that he is God
revealed in the flesh, a point which, I will argue later, Warfield
develops in a deep and profound manner. This, of course, requires that the fulness of God be indwelling Christ, and this, in
turn, strikes at the very heart of the kenotic theory. Put simply,
a God divested of his attributes in an incarnation is not a God
manifested as God in the flesh. It is a God manifested as something less than God in the flesh. Such an incarnation is therefore
no adequate revelation of God. This is one of the amazing facts
about Christ: that in him all the fulness of the godhead is seen
dwelling in bodily form. Anything less destroys his glory. The
kenotic theory therefore offers an inadequate understanding
of what the Incarnation is and thus makes the Incarnation a
thoroughly inadequate basis for any knowledge of God. If the
theory is motivated by a desire to preserve the unity of Christ's
person, or his identification with humanity, it does so only at
the incalculably high theological price of separating God as he
manifests himself from God as he is in himself. In other words,
the Incarnation is no longer revelation.

   It is at this point that I must register my disagreement with
the comments on Warfield by John Murray in the review of
The Person and Work of Christ which originally appeared in the
Westminster Theological Journal and was is reproduced in volume
three of the *Collected Writings*.[15] In this review, Murray claims to

---

14. *The Person and Work of Christ*, 46.
15. John Murray, *Collected Writings* , III, 358-61.

see a discrepancy between Warfield's rejection of kenoticism
in the article cited above and his statements in one of the sermons appended to the essays. Now, before examining Murray's
point, we should note that he sees the conflict not as an act of
self-contradiction but as the result of Warfield changing his
mind: the article was published in 1915, and Murray postulates
that the sermon is of an earlier date, representing therefore an
earlier phase in Warfield's thinking. The sermon certainly was
of earlier provenance, appearing in the 1913 volume entitled *The
Saviour*, which was dedicated to the Faculty of Theology at the
University of Utrecht in gratitude for the award of an Honorary
Doctorate in Theology.[16] Nevertheless, it is my contention that
there is no contradiction between the sermon and the article,
and that we need not therefore impute a tacit change of mind
to Warfield on this issue.

The two offending statements by Warfield read as follows:

> It was although He was in the form of God, that Christ Jesus did
> not consider His being on an equality with God so precious a pos-
> session that He could not lay it aside, but rather made no account
> of Himself.[17]

And:

> Did Christ stand upon His unquestioned right of retaining His
> equality with God?[18]

From these sentences, Murray draws the following conclusion:

> [T]he obvious implication ... [is] that, in Warfield's esteem, Christ
> divested Himself of His equality with God.[19]

Were this the case, then this would reveal that a most significant
development in Warfield's Christology had taken place between

---

16. *The Saviour* has been reprinted by Banner of Truth.
17. The original is found in *The Person and Work of Christ*, 570.
18. *The Person and Work of Christ*, 572.
19. John Murray, *Collected Writings*, III, 360.

1913 and 1915. Indeed, it would necessitate that he had moved from a kenotic position to a classically orthodox position, and this in itself would raise fascinating questions regarding the influences at work on him and the processes of his thought during this time. Several factors militate against this, however, which I believe decisively demonstrate continuity on this issue in his writings.

First, a general comment: we should note that Warfield's theology is first and foremost an exegetical theology; that is, it is a theology which seeks to expound scriptural revelation and to relate all of its claims to that revelation. Now this is not to say that his theology was simply the result of expounding biblical texts in some kind of presuppositionless vacuum. Not at all. Warfield came to the scriptures with the presupposition that orthodox Christianity, as expressed in the specific form of the historic Reformed confessions, was true. To say that his theology is first of all exegetical is, however, to make the point that he was willing to run risks with language, so to speak, providing that the choice of language was allowed by scripture. Thus, when it came to the Incarnation, he was unwilling to allow his commitment to the New Testament theme of Christ as God manifest in the flesh and as the one in whom all the fulness of the Godhead dwelt in bodily form, to undermine equally biblical emphases. Far less would he allow the Chalcedonian definition to take on a life of its own and restrict what even the Bible has to say about the Incarnation. Now, we do have to be careful here, particularly at the present time – much rubbish is spouted today about 'tensions' and 'paradoxes' in the Bible's teaching which, while sometimes valid, is often an excuse for a lack of hard wrestling with the Bible's teaching. What I do not wish to imply is that Warfield was willing to offer a position whereby Christ both did and did not divest himself of his divine attributes at one and the same time. Such a 'paradox' might appeal, but it is ultimately nonsense. Rather, I wish to make the point that Warfield's Christology was driven by the need to make sense of the biblical accounts of the person and work of Jesus Christ of Nazareth.

The second point to make, and the one which counts decisively against John Murray's interpretation of Warfield, is that
precisely the same language to which Murray objected in the
sermon is actually used in the article to which he is referring.
I quote the relevant passage at length:

> His earthly life is...distinctly represented as a humiliation. Though
> even on earth He is one with the Father, yet he 'descended' to
> earth; He had come out from the Father and out of God; a glory
> had been left behind which was yet to be returned to, and His
> sojourn on earth was therefore to that extent an obscuration of
> His proper glory. There was a sense, then, in which, because He
> had 'descended,' He was no longer equal with the Father...because
> of the humiliation of His present condition, and in so far as this
> humiliation involved entrance into a status lower than that which
> belonged to Him by nature.[20]

Given all that is said elsewhere in this article, this humiliation
is clearly no divestment of divine attributes in a sense which
somehow separated Christ from God or made him less than God
in the Incarnation. Rather, it is to be understood in line with
classic Reformed orthodoxy on the Incarnation in terms of the
voluntary functional subordination of the Son to the Father in
the economy of salvation, and of the assumption of human nature, involving as this did exposure to human limitations such as
hunger, thirst and physical tiredness. If Warfield had exhibited
the same nervousness about the language of humiliation which
John Murray's comments betray, it is arguable he could not have
stood so solidly within the Reformed tradition on this issue, nor
done subsequent justice to the biblical teaching about Christ's
humanity and its relationship to his divine nature.

This brings us neatly to the next point I wish to make about
Warfield, and that is his usefulness as a theologian who reflected
in great depth upon the significance of Christ's humanity. If he
rejected the various kenotic theories as inadequate, this was
not at the expense of playing down or marginalising Christ's

---

20. *The Person and Work of Christ*, 61.

humanity. Rather, he stands out within the Reformed tradition as one who expended an exceptional amount of energy reflecting upon Christ's humanity, something which no doubt derived from his desire to be first and foremost an exegetical theologian who wished to do justice to the Gospel accounts of Christ. It is perhaps arguable that, in terms of biblical texts, evangelical Protestantism has focused largely upon the letters of Paul and not so much upon the historical narratives of the Gospels. This kind of theological culture can sometimes give the impression that the death and resurrection of Christ are the only significant things in his ministry and, if we are honest, can perhaps leave many believers unsure as to why exactly we have four Gospels, when the letters of Paul and the Gospel of John seem to provide us with all the theology that we need. The Gospels give us some heart-warming anecdotes, but are they really important? Such a culture, betrays, I think, a failure to reflect properly upon Christ's humanity, and in this context, the work of Warfield is most instructive.

The Humanity of Christ
It is the motif of humiliation noted above, with its counterpart of exaltation, which is crucial to Reformed understandings of Christ's person. As we might therefore expect, this lies at the heart of Warfield's own ability to do full justice to the humanity of Christ. It developed within Reformed theology as a means of expressing the dynamic nature of Christ's life on earth and, therefore, as a way of expressing the importance not simply of his death and resurrection but of his whole life as a revelation of God's grace and as constitutive of the way of salvation. Summarising the Reformed tradition on this issue, Louis Berkhof divides humiliation into two components, self-emptying and then voluntary subjection to the law, and five stages, incarnation, suffering, death, burial, and descent into hell. Christ's exaltation thus begins with the resurrection.[21] The strength of this theological structure is both its sensitivity to

---

21. Berkhof, 332.

the historical movement involved in Christ's saving work, and in the convenient way in which it allows for careful emphasis to be placed upon the fact that Christ is God *manifest in the flesh*, that is, God made present in humanity under the conditions of space and time.

From the very early days of the Christian church, the attack on the reality of Christ's humanity had been a central concern. Various early heresies exhibited docetic tendencies – that is, the idea that Christ's humanity was a mere appearance, something which merely 'seemed' to be real human flesh and bone. The church responded by vigorously asserting the reality of Christ's humanity and in one of the earliest traditional statements of Christian faith, the so-called 'Rule of Faith', much was made of the need to maintain the reality of Christ's historical, physical person. Indeed, it was the early church father, Gregory of Nazianzus, who put the issue with force and clarity: what was not assumed was not redeemed. The implication is obvious: if Christ did not assume humanity, then humanity has not been saved.

Having said all this, I suspect that many of us are probably much more comfortable and clear about the implications of Christ's divinity than we are about those of his humanity. Even John Murray, it would seem, was uneasy with Warfield's robust language regarding Christ's humiliation, and yet Warfield stood clearly within the trajectory of expression stemming from the Bible's own words and thoroughly approved of by the majority Reformed tradition. Nevertheless, there is something in this blunt talk of humiliation, of subordination, and of limitation which leaves us fearful for the integrity of Christ's divinity.

The most brilliant and extended treatment which Warfield gives to Christ's humanity is the remarkable essay, 'The Emotional Life of Our Lord'.[22] Warfield starts the essay with a comment that is so straightforward and yet absolutely explosive in its implications: 'It belongs to the truth of our Lord's humanity, that he was subject to all sinless human emotions.'[23] Such

22. *The Person and Work of Christ*, 93-145.
23. *The Person and Work of Christ*, 93.

a comment serves as an immediate warning to any who might disparage the importance of the topic or shy away from discussion in this area out of some specious modesty. Warfield's point is simple: the existence of Christ as a human being means that he is fully human in every sense of the word; and that means we must understand him as an emotional being, albeit without sin. By implication, to do anything less is to be guilty of an incipient docetism which threatens the very reality of the Incarnation.

It is perhaps indicative of precisely this tendency in Reformed thought – or, perhaps, more charitably, of a zeal to protect Christ's divinity – that there is very little reflection upon Christ's emotional life within the tradition. Indeed, this article of Warfield would appear to be the only substantial piece devoted exclusively to this theme available in the literature. Louis Berkhof, while not being a great constructive theologian, is nevertheless an excellent summariser of the tradition. His *Systematic Theology* is therefore a relatively reliable guide to the emphases and concerns of Reformed thinking. On this issue of Christ's emotional life, with the exception of the inevitable short section on Christ's sufferings, he has nothing to say. Yet this is surely a most serious theological lacuna: if Christ is truly human, then that requires that he had an emotional life; if the biblical accounts of Christ are accurate, they require that he had an emotional life; and if the Reformed faith is to paint a fully orbed picture of Christ, it must give due attention to this area.

Warfield prefaces his analysis of Christ's emotions by pointing out that we cannot presuppose in advance that all emotions ascribed to Christ are to be ascribed simply to his human nature. Warfield allows that this may be the case, but will not go so far as to say that it *must* be so. Instead, he proposes his essay simply as a clarification of which emotions are ascribed by the Gospel narratives to Christ's person, in the hope that others will develop the argument further (a hope which seems, at the present time, to have remained unfulfilled).[24]

---

24. *The Person and Work of Christ*, 94-96.

The emotions which Warfield sees ascribed to Christ are as follows: compassion, love, anger, sorrow, joy, anguish, and indignation. What is so striking about this approach of Warfield is the way in which it anchors our understanding of these emotions in a firmly concrete setting. Abstraction has been a constant temptation for theologians over the years, whereby a particular concept takes on a life of its own and comes to exert a decisive influence over the way in which the Bible is understood. Thus, notions of wrath or love are divorced from their setting in the biblical materials, distorted, and then read back into the Bible in a manner which damages its message. We can all probably think of examples. Holiness is a classic, where, many times over the centuries it has become identified with certain cultural peculiarities rather than with the biblical notion of exclusive devotion or separation to a particular object. Thus, in the Middle Ages, holiness became identified with a particular kind of contemplative existence set within the context of a celibate life. Then, in later Protestantism, holiness came to be identified with abstention from various things, whether tobacco, alcohol, or the theatre. Now, do not misinterpret me here: I am arguing neither for nor against the appropriateness of these particular examples; all I wish to point out is that the abstraction of concepts such as holiness from their place in the biblical narrative leads to distorted and reductionist understandings of what these terms mean.

Protestantism was, at its very inception, a revolt against precisely this kind of theological abstraction. In his famous 'theology of the cross', Martin Luther argued that the problem with medieval theology had been that it had taken notions of, say, love, power, and holiness from the world around it and had imposed them upon the Bible. For Luther, this was simply idolatry. Against this, Luther argued that if we wished to know how these terms applied to God, then we had to look to where God had revealed their meaning. In other words, if we want to know what God is like, then we must look to where God has revealed himself. For Luther, this revelation was on the cross: thus, God's power was revealed not in some superhuman strength but in his weakness; his love through making himself despised; and his holiness through being outwardly cursed and abandoned.

Now, many of us today would hesitate to go all the way with Luther's theology of the cross for a variety of reasons; but the basic principle, that God is who he has revealed himself to be and not who we necessarily expect him to be, is good and sound. It is in this context that Warfield's approach to the emotional life of Christ is so useful.

Let us take, for example, the issue of divine anger. There are, of course, many today who disparage the notion of divine anger. Some do so from an avowedly liberal attitude to the biblical text, wherein the anger of God is seen as a reflection of certain cultural or psychological influences on the writers and as having no real reference to any God 'out there' so to speak. There are, however, many who claim to take the biblical record seriously who doubt that the language of wrath and anger is meant to be taken in any literal or personal sense but is rather to be seen as a metaphorical reference to the impersonal though unfortu- nate results of sin. Thus, if we play with fire, we inevitably get burned – nothing personal, so to speak, merely the necessary consequence of ignoring the maker's instructions.

I would suggest at this point that an examination of wrath and anger in terms of Christology might well offer a rather dif- ferent picture of divine wrath. Let me quote a couple of passages from Warfield. The first refers to the cleansing of the Temple:

> Perhaps in no incidents recorded in the Gospels is the action of our Lord's indignation more vividly displayed than in the accounts of the cleansings of the Temple. In closing the account which he gives of the earlier of these, John tells us that 'his disciples remem- bered that it was written, The zeal of thine house shall eat me up' (John 2:17). The word here employed – 'zeal' – may mean nothing more than 'ardor'; but this ardor may burn with hot indignation, – we read of a 'zeal of fire which shall devour the adversaries' (Heb. 10:27). And it seems to be this hot indignation at the pollu- tion of the house of God – this 'burning jealousy for the holiness

of the house of God' – which it connotes in our present passage....
The form in which it here breaks forth is that of indignant anger
towards those who defile God's house with trafficking, and it
thus presents us with one of the most striking manifestations of
the anger of Jesus.[25]

The most obvious point to make about Warfield's comment
is that he has himself picked up on the most glaringly obvious
point of the original biblical account: Christ's anger or indignation in this context is personal and active. We are not dealing
here with the impersonal and mechanistic outworking of the
moral laws of the universe; no – we are dealing with a God who
is outraged at the wicked actions of certain of his creatures, and
who takes positive action in response to this sin. Word studies,
clever exegesis of various 'wrath' passages, and philosophical
reflection may well be used in an attempt to sidestep the traditional church teaching on divine wrath, but the cleansing of
the Temple provides us with an actual incident which makes
such manoeuvres somewhat less than convincing. Here is God
manifest in the flesh actually expressing anger against those who
buy and sell in the house of the Lord. This is real personal anger
which finds its outworking in real personal action on the part
of Christ. And when all is said and done, Christian theology is
rooted not in metaphysical abstractions but in the revelation of
God. It is here that Warfield's focus on Christ as fully incarnate,
and thus as an emotional being, is so useful in the struggle for
biblical orthodoxy because it takes the notion of the wrath of
God and makes it a personal category, linking it to the action
of a real person in space-time history.

Lest, however, this be seen as generating a picture of God as
hard and unyielding, albeit personal and active, it is worth quot-
ing a second passage from Warfield's article, this time focusing
on Christ's anger outside of the tomb of Lazarus:

Inextinguishable fury seizes him.... It is death that is the object of
his wrath, and behind death him who has the power of death, and

---

25. *The Person and Work of Christ*, 121.

whom he has come into the world to destroy. Tears of sympathy may fill his eyes, but this is incidental. His soul is held by rage: and he advances to the tomb, in Calvin's words again, 'as a champion who prepares for conflict.' The raising of Lazarus thus becomes, not an isolated marvel, but – as indeed it is presented throughout the whole narrative...a decisive instance and open symbol of Jesus' conquest of death and hell. What John does for us in this particular statement is to uncover to us the heart of Jesus, as he wins for us our salvation. Not in cold unconcern, but in flaming wrath against the foe, Jesus smites in our behalf. He has not only saved us from the evils which oppress us; he has felt for and with us in our oppression, and under the impulse of these feelings has wrought our redemption.[26]

The passage is powerful indeed, for it allows Warfield to bring out the anger and the fury which Christ feels when confronted with the outrageous wages of sin, and allows us to see that salvation is not simply some abstract metaphysical concept but goes to the very heart of God's being. Salvation is the result of God's compassion for sinners and his anger at the impact of sin. As he cleared the Temple of those who had changed the house of God into a market-place, so he fights against sin as that which has marred his creation and turned it into a nightmare – and he does this with an anger and a fury that befits the Lord of the universe.

The drama of these two incidents brings home the nature of God's anger against sin in a far more rich and striking way than any abstracted talk of God's wrath might do; and Warfield's concern to do justice to the fact of the Incarnation, to Christ as God manifest in the flesh, allows him to bring out this truth with force. If the evangelical world can often seem to be polarised between an attitude to God's wrath which virtually disposes of the idea and one which makes it so overwhelming and awesome that it seems impossible to square with any meaningful notion of God's love, then I would suggest that further reflection upon the lines laid down by Warfield in his discussion of Christ's emotions might well bear significant fruit.

---

26. *The Person and Work of Christ*,117.

One final example can be offered to help to reinforce this point: Warfield's comments on Christ's compassionate cries over Jerusalem. This is precisely the kind of text where one might expect a theologian to address the knotty issues of the relationship between Christ's divine and human natures; but Warfield does not do so, preferring to see the passage not as a problem for Christology but as a deep revelation of the heart of God as he manifested himself in Christ. Listen to what he says:

> We may...place the loud wailing over Jerusalem and the deep sighing over the Pharisees' determined opposition side by side as exhibitions of the profound pain given to our Lord's sympathetic heart, by those whose persistent rejection of him required at his hands his sternest reprobation. He 'sighed from the bottom of his heart' when he declared, 'There shall be no sign given to this generation'; he wailed aloud when he announced, 'The days shall come upon thee when thine enemies shall dash thee to the ground.' It hurt Jesus to hand over even hardened sinners to their doom. It hurt Jesus, – because Jesus' prime characteristic was love, and love is the foundation of compassion.[27]

Here again we see Warfield using the historical account of Jesus Christ of Nazareth to bring depth and substance to a divine attribute, namely, that of compassion. We could spend hours discussing the definition of compassion, of elaborating on what it may or may not involve – but here, by going straight to a concrete act of the real person, Jesus Christ of Nazareth, the full glory of God's compassion for humanity is brought out in startling relief. Here we see God weeping over the lost; here we see God saddened by the plight of sinful humanity; here we see God's heart broken by the stubbornness of a world that has gone to the bad.

This brings us back, of course, to the problem with kenotic Christology. If God divests himself of his attributes in the incarnation, if we have in Jesus of Nazareth God reduced and hidden in the flesh rather than manifest in the flesh, then these

---

27. *The Person and Work of Christ*, 101.

acts of Christ do not really give us insight into the psychology and thoughts of God at all. The anger might be the result of God having cast off his ability to control himself; the weeping at Lazarus's tomb might be the shocked response of one who was unaware of the enormity of sin and the scale of the task which he faced; and the cries over Jerusalem might say more about Christ's self-imposed impotence in the face of sin than about his deep-seated compassion for even the most hardened sinners. It is only his firm commitment to the Christology of Chalcedon and his refusal to go down the seductive but ultimately self-defeating path of kenoticism that allows Warfield to mine the full riches of the New Testament portrait of Christ. I end this section with a passage from another essay by Warfield which brings this point home:

> The Jesus of the New Testament is not fundamentally man, however divinely gifted: he is God tabernacling for a while among men, with heaven lying about Him not merely in His infancy, but throughout the days of His flesh.[28]

Building on the Foundation

Where, then, does all this fairly abstruse and sophisticated theology lead? What, in modern parlance, is the cash-value of what Warfield has to say? There are many points I could make here, but I close with just two.

First, Warfield clearly shows that a commitment, a true, thoughtful commitment, to the traditional understanding of Christ as God manifested in the flesh should make all of our theology, and thus all of our lives, Christ-centred. By realising that Christ is not simply an instrument by which God achieves his salvific purposes but is himself God manifest in the flesh, a revelation of the deepest, innermost being of God himself, then our knowledge of who God is and of how he thinks should be revolutionised. Too often, I suspect, we think of God in abstract terms; too often we perhaps reduce him to a set of laws or some

---

28. *Works*, III, 163.

impersonal principle which controls the universe. But he is not like that. He is personal and he has feelings of love towards his creatures and anger towards sin. This is not to reject the orthodox notions of his immutability; it is simply to draw out the revelation of God in Christ. Preachers should not be frightened of teaching their people that God is personal with feelings, for to neglect this is to neglect a central part of the Bible's own teaching and to deny revelatory value to the Incarnation. As Warfield himself declares:

> We have a God who is capable of self-sacrifice for us. It was although he was in the form of God, that Christ Jesus did not consider his being on an equality with God so precious a possession that he could not lay it aside, but rather made no account of himself. It was our God who so loved us that he gave himself for us. Now, herein is a wonderful thing. Men tell us that God is, by the very necessity of his nature, incapable of passion, incapable of being moved by inducements from without; that he dwells in holy calm and unchangeable blessedness, untouched by human sufferings or human sorrows.... Let us bless God that it is not true. God can feel; God does love. We have scriptural warrant for believing, as it has been perhaps somewhat inadequately but not misleadingly phrased, that moral heroism has a place within the sphere of the divine nature.[29]

The second application is the value of the Incarnation as a pattern of service. The Reformed world today is one of power struggles, where factions vie with each other for control of institutions, of pulpits, of printing presses. Yet Warfield calls us back to the Incarnation as an example that undermines all of our petty pride and scheming. Because Christ is God manifest in the flesh, we are, says Warfield, called upon to imitate him. Now, this imitation is clearly not absolute: Christ is unique in that he is God; we, as mere humans and humans alone, cannot imitate the Incarnation in the profoundest sense of the word. But the condescension involved in the Incarnation, the self-

---

29. *The Saviour*, 261-62.

denial, the love, the sacrifice, the willingness to give oneself for
the benefit of another, these are all elements that we are com-
manded to imitate. It is in this self-denial that the Christian
finds himself living out the true Christian life, and it is perhaps
fitting that we close this lecture by allowing Warfield again to
speak for himself. His ethic is no sterile moralism; rather, it is an
ethic which rises as a command from out of his understanding
of Christ as God Incarnate, manifests itself in love to others,
and flows back to Christ as the grateful response of redeemed
humanity to the God who saves:

> Only, when we humbly walk this path, seeking truly in it not our
> own things but those of others, we shall find the promise true, that
> he who loses his life shall find it. Only, when, like Christ, and in
> loving obedience to his call and example, we take no account of
> ourselves but freely give ourselves to others, we shall find, each in
> his measure, the saying true of himself also: 'Wherefore also God
> hath highly exalted him'. The path of self-sacrifice is the path to
> glory.[30]

---

30. *The Saviour*, 270.

SIX

IS THE FINNISH LINE A NEW BEGINNING? A CRITICAL ASSESSMENT OF THE READING OF LUTHER OFFERED BY THE HELSINKI CIRCLE*

The 1998 collection of essays on the Finnish perspective on Luther, edited by Carl Braaten and Robert Jenson, is both a fascinating contribution to modern ecumenical debates and an interesting challenge to accepted interpretations of Luther's theology. Many of the issues raised are extremely complex and a short paper such as this cannot aspire to do much more than offer a few passing comments and criticisms on the whole.[1]

The context of the collection is the ecumenical dialogue between the Evangelical Lutheran Church of Finland and the Russian Orthodox Church.[2] While we must beware of reading too much significance into this context in terms of research outcomes, it undoubtedly shapes the contours of debate in which the protagonists engage. Tuomo Mannermaa and his colleagues in the 'Helsinki Circle' are clearly driven by a desire to find in Luther's writings more ecumenical potential with reference to Lutheran-Orthodox relations than has typically been assumed to be available. That the research of the Finns has borne just such fruit, and is significant precisely because it is pragmatically so useful for ecumenical relations, is confirmed with great and

---

*This chapter originally appeared as an article in the *Westminster Theological Journal* (Volume 65, 2003). I am grateful to Professor Timothy Wengert, of The Lutheran Theological Seminary at Philadelphia, for reading and commenting on an earlier draft of this paper; also to my research assistant, Mr Brandon Withrow, for tracking down various relevant items of secondary literature.

1. Carl E. Braaten and Robert W. Jenson, *Union with Christ: the New Finnish Interpretation of Luther* (Grand Rapids: Eerdmans, 1998).
2. Tuomo Mannermaa, 'Why is Luther So Fascinating? Modern Finnish Luther Research,' *Union with Christ*, 1-20, esp. 1.

unmitigated enthusiasm by Robert Jenson in his own response to the group's work.[3]

Without wishing to endorse all of the enthusiasm which surrounds the Helsinki Circle, I would like to note at the start a number of observations at which this group makes extremely valid points and thus renders a useful contribution to the wider field of Luther interpretation. In the central contention that modern readings of Luther have been distorted by the use of an anti-ontological grid provided by the post-Kantian trajectories of German liberal theology, I think the writers do us a great service. The work of those under the sway of Ritschl and Holl comes in for some timely and necessary criticism. To a historian, it is obvious that Luther is operating within an intellectual framework shaped by the late medieval schools; the kind of anti-metaphysical thinking propounded by Kant and those who came after him is simply inappropriate as a framework for reading Luther's own writings. In addition, the kind of existentialist reading offered by Ebeling is equally damaging in its failure to understand the significance for Luther not simply of the force of language but also of the propositional content of the same. To the extent that these excesses of interpretation can only be corrected by an acknowledgment that Luther's view of the world was not that of a post-Kantian, the Finnish interpretation stands as a necessary corrective.[4]

---

3. 'I cannot respond to Tuomo Mannermaa's paper in the usual fashion: by first expressing appreciation and then registering reservations. For I have none of the latter.... My interest in Luther is not that of a *Lutherforscher*, but that of a systematic theologian and ecumenist. As a systematician, I have found that I can *do* very little with Luther as usually interpreted.' 'Response to Tuomo Mannermaa, "Why is Luther so fascinating?"' *Union with Christ*, 21-24, 21.

4. See Albrecht Ritschl, *Die christliche Lehre von der Rechtfertigung und Versöhnung*, 3 vols. (Bonn: A. Marcus, 1882-83); Karl Holl, *Luther* in *Gesammelte Aufsätze Kirchengeschichte* 1 (Tübingen: Mohr, 1927); Gerhard Ebeling, *Luther: an Introduction to his Thought* (Philadelphia: Fortress, 1970). For a recent defence of the Kantian interpretation of Luther over against the existentialism of Ebeling, see James M. Stayer, *Martin Luther, German Saviour: German Evangelical Theological Factions and the Interpretation of Luther, 1917-1933* (Montreal: McGill-Queen's, 2000).

Yet, while acknowledging the positive benefits of finding previously untapped ecumenical potential in the writings of Luther, a series of issues needs to be addressed before we can say with confidence and certainty that this Helsinki research represents a significant enrichment of the theological scene. Perhaps the most obvious question is that of the nature of the opinions of those who contribute to this volume. With the one exception, those responding to the Finns are entirely enthusiastic in what a cynic might consider to be a suspiciously uncritical manner. The collection would surely have been much stronger had there been more debate, more dissent and had more of the hard questions been asked and, hopefully, answered.[5]

Second, there is the obvious issue of the use of one man's writings as a basis for fruitful ecumenical dialogue. On the one hand, it is true that Luther does occupy a peculiar position within the Lutheran communion in a way that no single theologian does within either Reformed, Catholic or Orthodox traditions. Not only has he been an iconic figure and a rallying-point for group identity almost from the start, but his writings also carry official confessional weight.[6] Indeed, *The Formula of Concord* not only grants official confessional status to his Large and Small Catechisms but also commends all his other writings to the church, albeit in critical subjection to the word of God.[7] Thus, it is certainly legitimate to explore these writings as being of some ecumenical relevance. On the other hand, the methodological problems involved in such a task are at the very least utterly daunting. Luther lived a long life and wrote a huge amount in a wide variety of genres and contexts; in addition, his thinking

---

5. The one dissenting voice is that of Dennis Bielfeldt, 'Response to Sammeli Juntunen, "Luther and Metaphysics",' *Union with Christ*, 161-66.

6. On Luther's iconic influence in Lutheranism, see the stimulating study by Robert Kolb, *Martin Luther as Prophet, Teacher, and Hero: Images of the Reformer, 1520-1620* (Grand Rapids: Baker, 1999).

7. See Robert Kolb and Timothy Wengert (eds), *The Book of Concord: the Confessions of the Evangelical Lutheran Church* (Minneapolis: Fortress Press, 2000), 528-29. The confessional material also contains throughout explicit and repeated references to Luther and his writings.

underwent considerable development over time. The intellectual historian thus faces a vast array of preliminary methodological questions, such as: which texts do we privilege in our quest for the voice of the 'authentic' Luther? To what extent do we impose a coherence on Luther's thought, or at least upon its develop-ment over time, which will allow us to synthesise ideas in texts which are widely separated by chronological and/or generic context? Once one moves beyond the interpretative boundar-ies or trajectories set by the documents embodied in *The Book of Concord*, or, as do the contributors here, one assumes a basic disjunction to exist between the voice of the authentic Luther and the voice of the Lutheran confessional community as this finds public expression in the key creedal documents, one can-not avoid such sharp hermeneutical questions or be particularly surprised when others make accusations of selective reading of texts, projectionism and eisegesis.[8]

Third, and more substantively, there is the question of the historical accuracy of the picture of Luther presented. As a historian, my first question of this collection is not that of whether the new perspective offered is *useful* to ecumenical dialogue – that much is obvious from the collection itself – but whether this new perspective in fact represents a fair and proper interpretation of what Luther himself actually believed. Now, I appreciate that the systematic truth of a theological claim does not ultimately depend upon who, humanly speaking, is making the claim. That Luther says 'Such-and-such is the case,' is significant – his writings are, after all, mentioned in the Book of Concord as having important theological weight for the church's public confession of the faith. Yet in focusing so much upon the usefulness of this Finnish picture of Luther rather than upon its historical accuracy, the contributors to

8. On the various problems surrounding interpretation of ideas in historical context, I am indebted to the methodological writings of Quentin Skinner. On the issues of continuity, coherence and anachronism, see in particular the revised version of his classic essay, 'Meaning and Understanding in the History of Ideas,' in Quentin Skinner, *Visions of Politics I: Regarding Method* (Cambridge: Cambridge UP, 2002), 57-89.

this volume seem to want to have their cake and eat it at the same time. A systematic theological position which relies very heavily upon a particular reading of history as part of its basic case can – indeed, surely must – legitimately be called to account in relation to the historiography on which it is, in part, constructed and which forms an important part of the arguments' rhetorical force. This is the burden of the essay by the one dissenting voice in the volume, that of Dennis Bielfeldt, who sees the Finns as engaging in significant unhistorical theological eisegesis to make a sixteenth-century Luther fit a twentieth-century ecumenical encounter with Orthodoxy. It is therefore disconcerting that at least one reviewer has singled out this note of historical scepticism as being a 'worn out scholarly criticism'. Really? Then why do the contributors make so much of the historical validity of their reading of Luther? It is the contributors who have decided to play the historical card; they can hardly complain when others then call them to account on this score. While an accusation of anachronistic projectionism is indeed a two-edged sword, as likely again to cut the very one who wields it, nevertheless those systematicians who purport to build great castles on foundations laid down by historical figures must accept that historians at least have the right to expect them to be able to justify their understanding of these foundations with reference to the accepted canons of history and historical interpretation.[9]

It is on the historical front that this volume does not score as highly as it does on that of systematic construction. While the use of Ritschl and Holl as key opponents is legitimate, given their massive influence both theologically and historiographically in the late nineteenth and early twentieth centuries, the more recent and highly influential work of Heiko Oberman is entirely

---

9. Michael Plekon, review in *St Vladimir's Theological Quarterly* 44 (2000), 109-12. Other reviews include: Mason Beecroft and J. Scott Horrell, *Bibliotheca Sacra* 157 (2000), 250-51; Ted Dorman, *First Things* 98 (December 1999), 49-53; S M Hutchens, *Touchstone* 13.6 (2000), 41-46; Andriy Honcharuk, *Logia* 9 (2000), 45-47; James M. Kittelson, *Dialog* 38 (1999), 235-37.

absent from the discussion.[10] This is not incidental nor is it an irrelevant criticism; indeed, the omission is little short of stunning. The kind of historical method pioneered by Oberman, by his student, David Steinmetz, and by those who follow in their wake, such as Timothy Wengert, has stressed the need to set Luther's theological actions within both the synchronic and diachronic contexts in order to understand exactly what intentions, theological or otherwise, are being expressed in any given text, and why these are being expressed in the way they are.[11] It is not surprising, then, that in reviewing the volume in hand, Wengert in particular has been brutal in his criticisms of the lack of historical sensitivity and the failures to understand the wider context which the authors consistently exhibit.[12]

We should perhaps here take a number of examples. First, one of the collection's central claims is that union with Christ is the key to Luther's understanding of salvation, and that this union is something real and ontological which leads to a transformation of the believer akin to the Orthodox notion of theosis.[13] If true,

---

10. See Heiko A. Oberman, *Luther: Man between God and Devil*, ET E. Walliser-Schwarzbart (New Haven: Yale UP, 1989); also the essays on Luther in the following, *The Dawn of the Reformation* (Edinburgh: T. and T. Clark, 1992); *The Reformation: Roots and Ramifications* (Edinburgh: T. and T. Clark, 1994); and *The Impact of the Reformation* (Grand Rapids: Eerdmans, 1994).

11. See David C. Steinmetz, *Luther in Context* (Grand Rapids: Baker, 1995); Timothy J. Wengert, *Law and Gospel: Philip Melanchthon's Debate with John Agricola of Eisleben over Poenitentia* (Grand Rapids: Baker, 1997); idem, *Human Freedom, Christian Righteousness: Philip Melanchthon's Exegetical Dispute with Erasmus of Rotterdam* (New York: Oxford University Press, 1998).

12. See his review in *Theology Today* 56 (1999), 432-34: 'This volume presents readers with a perspective that is neither new nor, in final analysis, germane to the heart of Luther's theology. It is also not, as the preface boasts, radical. Instead it represents a debate with certain aspects of "German" theology. It ignores major schools of Luther interpretation.... [I]t glosses over the fact that Lutherans have been debating the question of justification among themselves since the sixteenth century.... Here one sees what happens when modern ecumenical agendas and old-fashioned pietism become the chief spectacles through which to view an historical figure.'

13. E.g., Mannermaa, 'Why is Luther so Fascinating?' 9-12; also his second essay, 'Justification and *Theosis* in Lutheran-Orthodox Perspective,' *Union with Christ*, 25-41.

this claim distances the thought of Luther from the confessional formulation of justification, with its overarching emphasis upon declarative and forensic categories and its transformation (so many opponents would claim) of the whole matter into a legal fiction.[14] The claim can be broken down into two parts: first, that Luther's language, or way of expressing salvation differs somewhat from that of the confessional materials; and, second, that this difference represents a basic discontinuity of theological substance. As such, this goes well beyond the more modest (and, in my opinion, legitimate) ambition of demonstrating the distorted nature of post-Kantian readings of Luther; it serves to attenuate or even to sever Luther's connection to the Lutheran church on one, if not *the*, central point of that communion's confession, namely, the issue of justification.

A few comments are in order here. First, there is no doubt that in, say, *The Freedom of the Christian Man*, Luther's preferred analogy for justification is not so much the courtroom as the marriage union of bride and groom. While it is true that the analogy does involve a certain legal dimension – for example, the 'joyful exchange' of property which takes place within marriage occurs partly because of the legal framework which defines the union – we should not overplay this. Union with Christ is indisputably part and parcel of Luther's approach to justification, and this has a variety of roots and connotations, not all of them by any means legal.[15] To acknowledge this, however, is not to concede the case to the Finns. After all, the meaning of 'union with Christ' is not a universal given. Marriage union, legal union, ontological union – all offer models of understanding the idea which may well differ in significant ways. Thus, the Finnish case rests not so much upon the idea that union with Christ is central to Luther's articulation of justification but rather upon the use of realistic language to describe the union and its effects. Mannermaa, for example, insists on discussing union with Christ by using language of

---

14. E.g., *The Formula of Concord*, chapter 3 in Kolb and Wengert, 562-63.

15. See the essay by Oberman, '*Simul Gemitus et Raptus*: Luther and Mysticism,' in idem, *The Dawn of the Reformation*, 126-54.

'participation in God', phraseology which, of course, brings with
it a large amount of theological baggage which may or may not
be appropriate to Luther. Thus, he claims:

> The core of Luther's concept of participation finds expression in
> the notion of the 'happy exchange,' according to which Christ takes
> upon himself the sinful person of the human being and bestows his
> own righteous person upon the humanity. What takes place here
> between Christ and the believer is a communication of attributes
> or properties: Christ, the divine righteousness, truth, peace, joy,
> love, power, and life gives himself to the believer.[16]

What is puzzling about this particular claim is that the reference
provided to demonstrate that there is a 'real' absorption of Christ's
righteousness by the believer and of sin and death by Christ is a
passage from Luther's lectures on Romans from 1515-16, dealing
with Romans 7:18. First, this is a rather early work upon which
to hinge an important argument about Luther's understanding of
justification and salvation. If, for the sake of argument, we allow
for the 'Reformation breakthrough' having occurred by this time
(and I myself reject such a claim), there is clearly huge intellectual
development between 1516 and 1520, let alone 1535, when the
great commentary on Galatians is published. Even if the text
says what Mannermaa claims (and that is a point I shall dispute
below), one wonders what the ultimate historical, theological
or ecumenical value of such a claim is. After all, the role of
humility in this work is also crucial to Luther's understanding
of salvation at this point – but that will very soon be abandoned
in favour of a single-minded focus on faith. A similar use of pre-
Reformation Luther occurs in two other essays. Juntunen's essay
on metaphysics and ontology depends heavily upon the Luther of
the middle years of the second decade of the sixteenth century;
and Peura uses the *Dictata super Psalterium* of 1513-16 to build much
of the foundation for his arguments about favour and gift, and
hinges the crucial arguments about theosis on this work. Indeed,
his essay title refers to 'Luther's understanding of justification'

---

16. 'Justification and *Theosis*,' 32.

in the singular, which, given the use of material from either side of the Reformation watershed on justification, is immediately suggestive of a systematic over-harmonization of the early Luther and the later Luther which does not do justice to the history of his intellectual development over time.[17] Further, the specific relation between contemporary systematic use of Luther's writings and the historical understanding of the development of his thought rears its head in a particularly acute form when the Finns use these early, pre-Reformation or transitional works as sources for Luther's normative theology; it is, to say the least, very disappointing that Mannermaa, Juntunen and Peura never address the kind of awkward issues of historical interpretation which such use raises.

To return, however, to Mannermaa's quotation from the Romans commentary: when read in the context in which the passage occurs, Luther is in fact not here discussing the joyful exchange of sins and righteousness as Mannermaa claims but rather the paradoxical reality of the believer being both old and new man; indeed, the passage contains no explicit reference to or discussion of the union between the believer and Christ and is simply not relevant to the argument Mannermaa is trying to make. In this passage, Luther is drawing an analogy between the believer as old and new man, and the paradoxical nature of Christology; the comparison is explicitly analogical, however, and in no way intended as a definitive explanation of the nature of union with Christ or of justification. To use the passage to argue for realistic union in the context of justification is entirely illegitimate, representing a clear misappropriation and misapplication of the passage.[18] Such a loose approach to the context

17. Simo Peura, 'Christ as Favor and Gift (*donum*): The Challenge of Luther's Understanding of Justification,' in *Union with Christ*, 42-69, esp. 50-51. Neither Peura, nor any of the other contributors, set Luther's use of the terminology of favour and gift against the contemporary theological or exegetical use of these terms.
18. See WA 56, 343, 16-21 (the text cited by Mannermaa). It is perhaps worth noting that, as the passage goes on, it refers to the unity produced by sexual intercourse but stresses that such unity is 'figurative', a somewhat less than ontological term: WA 56, 26-28.

of given statements from Luther is not an isolated occurrence in the essays in this volume.[19]

The Finnish case for real union does not, of course, rest solely upon this one misconstrued passage. Mannermaa uses the notion of 'participation' as a means of unlocking the theology of Luther's teaching on salvation from his early writings to the mature works of the 1530s.[20] While, on the surface, this appears to give unity to those writings which have traditionally been regarded as pre-Reformation or transitional and those which have been considered to be Reformation, it yet raises some crucial questions: what exactly is meant by, or results from, this 'participation'? And does participation play the central role in Luther's thinking which the Finns ascribe to it? Here we might look at Mannermaa's treatment of a later work: in discussing the importance of Christ as 'gift', Mannermaa quotes a passage from the 1535 *Commentary on Galatians* to the effect that the presence of Christ in the believer's heart as a gift is that which makes the Christian greater than the world. He then reads this passage as revealing 'how real (indeed, *ontologically* real [my emphasis]) Luther supposes the presence of the "gift," that is, Christ, to be.'[21] I would respond to such a reading in a number of ways. For a start, no attempt is made by the author to trace the meaning of the word 'gift' in the wider theological and exegetical context within which Luther is working, something which should be basic to any careful exegesis of his meaning at this point; the word has a significant exegetical and theological history, and is used after all by both Erasmus and Melanchthon – individuals

---

19. See the comments of Wengert: 'Countless times the present reviewer also encountered passages in Luther torn from their historical and exegetical contexts in order to serve greater ecumenical ends.... In short, this book will help readers to know what Finnish theologians think of their own tradition.' *Theology Today*, 434.

20. 'Justification and *Theosis*,' 25. See also the exchange in *Lutherjahrbuch* 66 (1999): Tuomo Mannermaa, 'Glaube, Bildung, und Gemeinschaft bei Luther,' 167-96; Eric W. Gritsch, 'Response to Tuomo Mannermaa,' 197-206; and Karl-Heinz zur Mühlen, 'Korreferat zu Tuomo Mannermaa,' 207-18.

21. 'Justification and *Theosis*,' 33. The quotation is from WA 40.1, 235, 26-236,16.

whose work is scarcely incidental to Luther's own – and chosen because of its wider connotations; it is therefore not simply a neologism or an empty bucket into which Luther can pour whatever content he wishes. Yet the reader of this volume looks in vain for any discussion which might help to contextualise and to clarify Luther's use of this terminology.

Second, even taken in isolation from the wider linguistic and theological context, the passage as presented does not self-evidently point towards an ontological reading, at least not one that tends in the direction of an Orthodox notion of theosis. All the passage says is that believers who have Christ as gift by faith in their hearts have consciences which are rendered free of all laws and subject to nothing. And this, after all, is central to Lutheran concepts of forensic justification, where God, the judge, declares the individual to be innocent *in foro conscientiae*.

In order to find out what Luther is really saying here, it is useful to look at the preface to the commentary, where he makes a number of crucial theological distinctions which serve to provide a framework for understanding the argument of the whole.[22] These are a twofold understanding of righteousness and a corresponding two kingdoms understanding of the reality in which the believer must live. As to twofold righteousness, Luther distinguishes between that which is passive and that which is active. The passive is that which, quite literally, does nothing and thus receives Christ by faith alone; in this context, language of righteousness is to be understood of the heavenly realm, not of the earthly; were this not the case, the absolute distinction Luther makes between the heavenly and the earthly would be rendered meaningless.[23] We might add that this is also the framework within which later discussion in the commen-

---

22. For the preface, see WA 40.1, 39-52. This is crucial in summarizing the theological framework within which Luther understands the letter's teaching to be understood.

23. 'Haec est nostra theologia qua docemus accurate distinguere has duas iustitias, activam et passivam, ne confundantur mores et fides, opera et gratia, politia et religio.' WA 40.1, 45, 24-26.

tary concerning the nature of justification and righteousness must be understood. What is absolutely crucial is the fact that active righteousness, that which involves the believer in doing good works and in dealing with the earthly realm, is radically mediocre and provides no basis for the relationship between the believer and God. Moreover, it is utterly dependent upon the logically prior heavenly righteousness – that which is really of Christ and only of the believer by imputation through faith, as is elaborated in the commentary itself.[24] Luther's preface makes it quite clear that these distinctions provide the great framework for his understanding of the teaching of Galatians on justification and that to confuse the two kinds of righteousness involves a basic confusion of the two realms and constitutes a basic and fundamental category mistake. It is, to say the least, extremely surprising that Mannermaa makes no attempt to set the teaching he finds on righteousness in the main text of the *Commentary on Galatians* within the larger theological framework laid out in the preface. The two realms distinction, and the active and passive distinction, make Luther's teaching in the *Commentary on Galatians* so clear; and the failure of the contributors to the Finnish volume to bring out the significance of these and then to use them as Luther did, as the framework for understanding the relationship between Christ's righteousness and ours, is one of the major flaws in this collection. The obvious question is: if participation in Christ in a manner akin to theosis is so crucial

---

24. 'Nos vero quasi duos mundos constituimus, unum coelestem, alterum terrenum. In illos collocamus has duas iustitias disiunctas et inter se maxime distantes. Iustititia legis est terrena, de terrenis agit, per hanc facimus bona opera. Sed sicut terra non profert fructus, nisi prius irrigata et foecundata e coelo (Terra enim non potest iudicare, renovare et regere coelum, sed econtra coelum iudicat, renovat, regit, et foecundat terram, ut faciat quod Dominus iussit), ita per iustitiam legis multa faciendo nihil facimus et implendo legem non implemus, nisi prius sine nostro opere et merito iustificati simus per iustitiam christianam nihil pertinentem ad iustitiam legis seu ad iustitiam terrenam et activam. Ista autem est iustitia coelestis et passiva quam non habemus, sed e coelo accipimus, non facimus, sed fide apprehendimus, per quam ascendimus supra omnes leges et opera.' WA 40.1, 46, 1930.

to Luther, why is there no major prolegomenal discussion of this in the preface to Galatians, and why is there so much discussion of these other distinctions?

Given this, the fact that Luther uses dramatically realist language to describe the presence of Christ at various points in the commentary does not require in any way an ontological reading à la Orthodoxy. Indeed, we know from elsewhere in Luther's writings that even the real presence of Christ does not require such an understanding: take, for example, the Lord's Supper, where Luther stresses the real presence of Christ yet where there is a deep sense in which the presence in the elements leaves the substance of those elements unchanged: they remain bread and wine even when Christ is really, sacramentally joined to them; indeed, the whole point is that the real presence of Christ in the elements does not lead to anything approaching a divinisation of the bread and the wine. Thus, to move from language which speaks of the real presence of Christ by faith in the believer to an understanding of salvation based upon some notion of transforming divinisation or theosis is a not inconsiderable leap and needs to be established on foundations of a contextual reading of the said language in the narrower context of the Luther texts within which it occurs and the wider theological and historical context of Luther's own life and work.

If one can object first, to the decontextual reading of the notion of gift, and, second, to the imputation of ontological significance to the passage where such is not required, my third objection is that the passage occurs in the heart of a section dealing precisely with imputation. In the previous paragraph, a Christian is defined as being not someone who feels no sin but someone to whom God does not impute sin because of faith in Christ and to whom Christ's righteousness is itself imputed, as a basis for justification and for the subsequent Christian life.[25]

25. 'Definimus ergo hunc esse Christianum, non qui non habet aut non sentit peccatum, sed cui illud a Deo propter fidem in Christum non imputatur. Ista doctrina affert firmum consolationem consientiis in veris pavoribus. Ideoque non frustra tam saepe et tanta diligentia inculcamus remissionem peccatorum et imputationem iustitiae propter Christum' WA 40.1, 235, 15-19.

Then, the following paragraphs make it clear that the kind of righteousness possessed by the believer through faith in Christ is absolutely discontinuous with any notion of intrinsic justifying righteousness, congruent or condign.[26] To describe the presence of Christ using ontological terminology is perhaps not incorrect, since Christ is indeed really present for Luther; but it is some-what confusing since this onto-logical presence is specifically understood in terms of its effects with reference to imputation and declaration, not first and fore-most of deification. Once more, had the important distinctions between active and pas-sive righteousness and earthly and heavenly realms been noted, Luther's meaning would have been clear. Moreover, as I shall argue below, the role of the two realms, the two righteousnesses and imputation here surely means that the kind of disjunction between Luther and the Lutheran confessions on this issue, if it exists at all, is really fairly small.

Of course, the Finnish Circle might well respond that imputa-tion, like union with Christ, is not a given and may have a variety of meanings which would allow for significant differences be-tween, say, Luther and Melanchthon, to be hidden or obscured by apparent verbal similarities. Yet again, it is worthwhile noting that the historical evidence points clearly towards substantial identity between the two men on this issue, despite attempts as far back as the Reformation, and more recently and most notably by Holl and his followers, to drive a substantial wedge between them on the issue of justification. A useful summary of the relationship between Luther and Melanchthon, theological and otherwise, and the history of the interpretation of that re-lationship by later scholars, is provided in an important article by Timothy Wengert.[27] In this, he points to the dependence of Luther upon Melanchthon on numerous issues; but, most significantly for the Finnish Circle, he also draws attention to a crucial letter from Melanchthon to Johannes Brenz, dated 12

---

26. WA 40.1, 236, 17-238, 19.

27. 'Melanchthon and Luther/Luther and Melanchthon,' *Lutherjahrbuch* 66 (1999): 55-88.

May 1531.[28] In this letter, Melanchthon lays out his forensic (*in foro conscientiae*) understanding of justification in contrast to Brenz's argument that it is the transforming or renewing work of the Holy Spirit which is the essence of the doctrine. In contrast to this, Melanchthon characteristically emphasizes the promise in Chirst as the basis for a good conscience before God.[29] Significantly, Luther adds a postscript to the letter in which, while offering a different emphasis to that of Melanchthon, one which focuses directly on Christ rather than on the promise, he yet makes the same point, implicitly affirming his colleague's position while expressing himself in slightly different terms. The language is different, the emphases are different, but at no point does Luther even hint at any real tension between his view and that of Melanchthon.[30] It is therefore clear that those who wish to drive a decisive wedge between Luther and Melanchthon, or between an alleged pristine view of justification as held by Luther and later alleged forensic perversion of the doctrine have some very difficult historical texts to deal with. My challenge to the Finns is: sure, imputation can be understood in a variety of ways; but, given the fact that Luther himself seems never to have had a major problem with Melanchthon's understanding, *on what basis can we legitimately read back into Luther's use of words such as 'imputation' any meaning which puts him at real odds with his younger colleague?*[31] In this volume, there is plenty of blunt assertion that there is a disjunction between Luther and Melanchthon/the later

28. *WA Br* 6, 98-101.

29. *WA Br* 6, 100, 25-29, 38-40.

30. *WA Br* 6, 100, 49-101. Luther's opening remarks are particularly clear (49-55): 'Et ego soleo, mi Brenti, ut hanc melius capiam, sic imaginary, quasi nulla sit in corde meo qualitas, quae fides vel charitas vocetur, sed in loco ipsorum pono Iesum Christum, et dico: Haec est iustitia mea, ipse est qualitas et formalis (ut vocant) iustitia mea, ut sic me liberem et expediam ab intuitu legis et operum, imo et ab intuitu obiectivi illius Christi, qui vel doctor vel donator intelligitur. Sed volo ipsum mihi esse donum vel doctrinam per se, ut omnia in ipso habeam.' Clearly, Luther sees his explanation as an alternative way of expressing the same doctrine as that offered by Melanchthon.

31. Cf. Luther's own appreciative attitude to Melanchthon's exegesis of Romans: *WA TR* 1, 139, 2-4; also Wengert, 'Melanchthon and Luther,' 65-66.

confessional trajectories, and not a little subtle insinuation to the same effect; but critical discussion of the crucial texts which might prove or disprove such a case is conspicuous only by its complete absence.

One might also add at this point that even in the Wittenberg of Luther's day, theological truth was not the preserve of one man who acted as unique source but was frequently the result of debate, public disputation, even conversations over good, German beer, and typical co-operation among colleagues. Indeed, it seems basic to the Finnish case that it is possible to isolate pure 'Luther theology' from the wider theological trajectories at Wittenberg, which reached back into the Middle Ages and the early Fathers, drank deep at the wells of Renaissance Humanism, interacted with wider contemporary opponents on the right and the left, and pushed forward to the confessional codifications which culminated in the Book of Concord. Such a position is, frankly, absurd, and cuts no scholarly ice with historians of the epoch.

Elsewhere in the article, Mannermaa proceeds to quote a number of further passages from the *Commentary on Galatians*, again stressing the centrality of union with Christ and again arguing that these indicate a strong ontological understanding of salvation which divides Luther from later Lutheranism because of his refusal to separate justification and sanctification.[32] This claim is highly problematic. It is quite clear that Luther works with a clear distinction between justification and what we might somewhat anachronistically call sanctification in the *Commentary*. For example, Luther explicitly makes imputation and the believer's possession of present perfect righteousness before God the basis for the subsequent performance of good works. There is no confusion of justification and what would later be called sanctification here; in fact, the two are clearly distinguished and the one is theologically subordinated to the other, albeit they are considered to be inseparable. That Luther does not embody this distinction in a specific conceptual vo-

---

32. 'Justification and *Theosis*,' 36-39.

cabulary is in itself of no substantial dogmatic significance as it is a linguistic commonplace that the possession of a concept is in no wise dependent upon the possession of a specific word for that concept.[33]

When we compare all this to the confessional material, nothing that Luther says in the *Commentary on Galatians* puts him at loggerheads with the teaching of the Augsburg Confession, where justification is clearly the result of God reckoning the believer righteous on the basis of faith.[34] Then, new obedience is seen to flow directly from this prior justification, while carefully distinguished from being either a basis, or a constitutive part, of righteousness before God.[35] There is nothing 'ontological' in any Eastern Orthodox sense of theosis in all this and, considering that the Augsburg Confession was composed during Luther's lifetime and enjoyed his full support, we would not, of course, expect to find major discontinuity between the thought of Luther and that of the confessional trajectory at this point. Furthermore, there seems to be little difference in real substance between the Augsburg Confession on these points and the Formula of Concord. It is true that the language of the Formula is more strident, more polemical – but this is explicable in terms of the changed ecclesiastical situation which required precisely such sharpening of language and definitions to maintain the legitimate trajectory of thought articulated by Luther in the *Commentary on Galatians* and made normative in the Augsburg Confession. Such an interpretation is entirely adequate and does not require the positing of a fundamental discontinuity or breach in the tradition which Luther apparently did not notice but which other approaches find necessary.[36] Further,

---

33. See WA 40.1, 233, 25-234, 23. Mannermaa comes close to conceding the essentially verbal nature of the difference at one point but still does not allow this to disturb his dogmatic interpretation: see 'Justification and Theosis,' 38.

34. Article 4: Concerning Justification; Kolb and Wengert, 38-41.

35. Article 5: Concerning the New Obedience; Kolb and Wengert, 40-41.

36. We might also add here the Schmalkaldic Articles, penned by Luther himself in 1537 and later incorporated into the Book of Concord. Again,

all of these confessional statements, one might add, presuppose precisely the same concepts of the two righteousnesses and the two kingdoms which we find in the preface to the *Commentary on Galatians* but which we do not find in the Finnish volume.[37]

Conclusion

This paper has been of necessity short, and many of the issues raised by the Finnish volume have not been touched upon. I can, however, summarise my preliminary criticisms as follows:

1. The Finnish volume, while making great play of building its arguments on historical texts, takes no account of major trajectories and methodologies of modern Luther scholarship. The absence of reference to the work of Oberman, Steinmetz and company, with their frank and legitimate stress upon the need to read Luther's works against the backgrounds of the exegetical and theological traditions to which they relate, leaves the volume historiographically very weak. Ideas of righteousness, gift and favour do not originate in a vacuum, and understanding their historical, intellectual, and exegetical background must form a necessary part of understanding how and why Luther is or is not using them.

2. The writers raise very legitimate questions about the hermeneutical framework imposed upon Luther's works by the Kantian and post-Kantian trajectories of Luther scholarship. They do not, however, raise the equally pressing problem of how the Luther canon should itself be read, and do not address the crucially important issue of historical development etc. within

---

these articles contain not a hint of the exposition of a specific ontology or of theosis as part of justification.

37. See Formula of Concord, chapter 3 and 4; Kolb and Wengert, 494-500; also the historical introduction, ibid., 481-85. On the development of confessional Protestantism in general, see Peter A. Lillback, 'Confessional Subscription Among Sixteenth Century Reformers,' in David W. Hall (ed.), *The Practice of Confessional Subscription* (Lanham: UPA, 1995); on specific controversies which led to a sharpening of the theological debates surrounding the role of works in the Lutheran tradition during Luther's own lifetime, see Wengert, *Law and Gospel, passim.*

Luther's own body of work. Thus, citations from pre-Reformation and Reformation works are routinely juxtaposed and synthesized in a manner which begs a huge number of questions about the validity of the method employed and the theological claims being made. One might add here that the virtually presupposed disjunction between Luther and the confessional trajectory (a contentious claim in itself) serves merely to exacerbate this as a methodological issue.

3. Examination of crucial texts in the Mannermaa article on theosis reveals a disturbing pattern of decontextual reading; and the emphasis upon participation combined with the failure throughout the volume to grasp the significance of the two righteousnesses and two kingdoms as basic elements of Luther's understanding of the Christian life leaves this reader at least unsatisfied that justice has really been done to the original theological content of the primary texts.

4. The disjunction that is driven between Luther and the confessional trajectory seems to require a distancing of Luther not only from the Formula of Concord but also from the Augsburg Confession. Such seems scarcely plausible, given Luther's stand towards the Augsburg Confession and, certainly, the evidence drawn from the 1535 *Commentary on Galatians* points in exactly the opposite direction to that which is claimed. If, as the Finns appear to want to do, one wishes to argue the inherently unlikely scenario that Luther's theology is closer to that of Gregory Palamas than to those confessions composed within his own lifetime by Wittenberg colleagues engaged in exactly the same theological, debates, discussions and projects as Luther, and with which he seems to have been quite satisfied, then the burden of proof *must* lie with the revisionists and not with the Reformation scholars. Why should we feel obliged to reinvent the wheel when it has not yet been demonstrated that the traditional design is seriously flawed? Indeed, there are numerous occasions in this volume when the references to the lectures on Romans and to the *Dictata* led me to wonder whether the Finns are actually opposing a pre-Reformation

Luther to a Reformation Luther. If such is the case, they have done little more than prove what we all knew all along: that Luther changes his mind in some significant ways on some very important issues. Of course, they might like to claim that Luther did not in fact change his mind significantly between 1513 and 1531; but then they have unfortunately (for them at least) to deal not simply with a mass of very carefully footnoted, thoroughly documented and tightly argued secondary scholarship which refutes such an idea (and is conspicuous in this volume only by its wholesale absence) but even with the very words and actions of Luther himself.

This again brings us back to the problem with which I started: what if Luther in his early years writes things which contradict the confessions? Not even in Lutheranism do these writings have the status accorded to the mature works and the church's more strictly confessional material. An ecclesiastical ecumenism built upon a selective reading from the whole of the Luther corpus seems doomed to achieve very little in terms of actual theological rapprochement. To build a systematic case on a reading of Luther which flies in the face of the most basic canons of historical method (reading texts in context, not isolating quotations in a manner which effectively subverts their meaning) might appeal to the most postmodern of minds but it should have no place at the table of reasoned ecumenism and honest, genuine, interconfessional dialogue.

PART TWO

SHORT, SHARP SHOCKS

ONE

THE IMPORTANCE OF EVANGELICAL BELIEFS

Perhaps the most important question facing evangelicals at the moment concerns the importance of evangelical beliefs – those propositions to which we assent – in the grand theological scheme. Are they merely reflections of our own religious aspirations? Are they simply one way of expressing a religious truth which can, in fact, be expressed in a variety of different ways? Or are they of the essence of the faith, to the extent that denial of certain beliefs is sufficient to render one outside of the bounds of historic, biblical Christianity? The question is all the more pressing, given the imperious demands of the postmodern, pluralist world within which we are frequently told that we all now live. For those of us committed to upholding the teaching of the UCCF doctrinal basis, and that in a manner consistent with the tradition of understanding epitomised by the great Christian creeds, the question of the importance of beliefs is, one would hope, unavoidable.

One of the most important books on this issue predates the whole postmodern issue, but still has much to say to us today. It is the little volume written by J. Gresham Machen in 1923 entitled *Christianity and Liberalism*. The book, a mere 189 pages (including index) in the Eerdmans edition on my shelf, is a passionate and cogently-argued plea for historic Christianity over against the liberal theology which Machen saw taking such a heavy toll upon the life and thought of the church in his day.

Central to Machen's case are two fundamental points. First, Christianity is built upon real, historical events, and when, for example, the Bible speaks of Christ's resurrection, it speaks of something which really happened to the incarnate God in space and time, not something which is simply a metaphorical reflection of the early church's religious experience of 'the Christ', whatever that term may itself be seen to symbolise. Second, doctrine matters – the historical events of God's dealings with people in history, and, supremely, his gracious saving action in Christ, have a universal significance which the church articulates through its doctrinal formulations founded on scripture. Thus, to say that Christ died is to state a historical fact; to say that Christ died for our sins is doctrine. History and doctrine are therefore bound together inseparably. Machen's own conclusion – dramatically stated yet one with which I find myself unable to disagree – is that, 'without these two elements [of history and of doctrine], joined in an absolutely indissoluble union, there is no Christianity.'

This basic point, the inseparability of faith and history, provides a vital touchstone for those engaged in the task of Christian theology. To abandon either is effectively to surrender the historic Christian faith, and – before anyone is tempted to dismiss Machen as an outdated fundamentalist – that is not simply the view of Machen, it is nothing less than the view the Bible itself expresses.

The lesson is a hard one – and particularly so for those of us, teachers and students, who live and work within the academic, scholarly environment. The separation of faith and history has become a basic axiom within certain traditions of theological endeavour, and this has inevitably spilled over into the wider church environment, where high profile church leaders have, over recent decades, made much play of denying that the question of the historicity of, say, the resurrection has any relevance to its theological significance. Nevertheless, we must be absolutely clear what is at stake here: the essence of Christianity itself. The historicity of an event like the resurrection is absolutely axiomatic to Christianity, and it is not just Machen who claims this, but no less than the Apostle Paul himself. One has only to turn to 1 Corinthians 15 to see what Paul regards as being the consequences of a denial of the resurrection: 'If there is no resurrection of the dead, then not even Christ has been raised. And if Christ has not been raised, our preaching is useless and so is your faith.' Paul goes on: if Christ is not raised then he, Paul, is a false witness, and, more than that, is to be pitied above all people as someone who has built his life upon a false hope. Paul regards the historical fact, the physical resurrection of Christ, and the doctrinal truth, the salvation and the general resurrection to which all believers look forward, as being bound so tightly together that one cannot deny the former without denying the latter.

This is hard teaching. At the very least it means that any system of thought which denies the historicity of the physical resurrection of Christ has effectively excluded itself from any right to the title of Christian. It is quite clear that Paul did not regard the difference between himself and those who denied the resurrection as one of a difference of emphasis or of two different approaches to Christianity. No. It was the difference between the true witness and the false witness, between those who have real Christian faith and those who do not. This is the point which Machen reaffirmed so eloquently in *Christianity and Liberalism*, and which we all, teachers and students alike, need to remind ourselves of again and again if we are to be faithful witnesses for Christ through our work.

This is not, of course, to argue that Christians should be obscurantist and not seek to interact with and even learn from those whose views are antithetical to the gospel. The best Christian theology has never taken refuge in a ghetto and engaged simply in a self-affirming monologue. The early church fathers, the great scholastics of the Middle Ages, the Reformers and, perhaps supremely, the Puritans all engaged with the wider intellectual environment. One has only to think of Augustine's use of Plato, Aquinas's interaction with Aristotle, Calvin's engagement with Cicero, and John Owen's interest in Maimonides to see that Christian orthodoxy has, at its best, always sought to engage with non-Christian thinking and even to appropriate such where this is possible without a basic betrayal of the gospel. The challenge today is to do the same, but to do it in a way that resists the almost unbearable pressures to blur the boundaries, which we all feel in a post-modern world that delights in pluralism, difference and its own peculiar brand of tolerance.

Such pressures come from a variety of sources. At one level, church politics make some of us unwilling to state the obvious concerning church leaders who deny the physical resurrection; at another level, the sheer amiable pleasantness of some theologians makes us feel awkward about criticising their views, lest we seem to have launched a narrow-minded personal attack on otherwise perfectly decent individuals; for the student, of course, the need to appease a supervisor who is, more than likely, hostile to orthodox Christianity, can prove an irresistible motive for cutting doctrinal corners; and for scholars, the need to get on in the academic community can be similarly seductive, especially today when evangelicalism can, with just a little modification and moderation, become in some contexts a good career move and buy itself a place at the postmodern table. Such pressures are not to be sniffed at and none of us can be complacent and trust in our own strength. This is why we must be quite clear about what is at stake: reputation, money, grades, position are all desirable – and none is wrong in and of itself – but at what cost? The unity of history and doctrine which lies at the heart of Paul's gospel does have eternal consequences – for those who affirm it and, let us not forget, for those who deny it; and to allow the fundamental legitimacy of the viewpoints of those who deny, for example, the physical resurrection, is in fact to make of ourselves false witnesses to the truth which all people, liberal theologians and radical church leaders as well as our next door neighbours, desperately need to hear. Christianity is a scandal – it is always going to be foolishness to those wise in their own wisdom – and we must be careful that credibility in whatever sphere we work in is not bought at the cost of evacuating Christianity of precisely those scandalous elements which constitute its very essence, whether by linguistic shifts such as that from 'resurrection' to 'Easter event' (as pointed out by Gerald Bray in a recent *Themelios*), or by the admiration, endorsement or uncritical appropriation of the views of those who think nothing of denying the very foundations of the faith.

As a postscript to these thoughts, I append a personal anecdote: a friend and I had the privilege recently of spending a week teaching and preaching in Romania. On the Sunday I had lunch with an old man on a small farm in the country. Over dinner it emerged that he had spent five years down the uranium mines under the communist regime for his Christian beliefs – for his conviction that Christ died on the cross and rose again. It is strange, but as he told me his story, neither church politics, nor personal reputation, nor academic credibility seemed quite so important any more. For some people the price of faithfulness is somewhat higher than it is for church leaders, academics, and students in the UK. Needless to say, I did not have to ask that man whether evangelical beliefs were important or not. Beliefs do matter – especially the scandalous ones – and we must beware of striving to make our evangelicalism too respectable.

TWO

WHAT CAN MISERABLE CHRISTIANS SING?

Many of us despise the health, wealth, and happiness teachings of the American televangelists and their pernicious British counterparts, as scandalous blasphemy. The idea that Christianity, at whose centre stands the Suffering Servant, the man who had nowhere to lay his head, and the one who was obedient to death – even death on the cross – should be used to justify the idolatrous greed of affluent Westerners simply beggars belief. Indeed, so contemptible is this school of thought that I will not waste precious column inches in *Themelios* by dignifying it with a reasoned response.

Nevertheless, there is a real danger that these heretical teachings have seeped into evangelical life in an imperceptible yet devastating way, affecting not so much our theology as our horizons of expectation. We live, after all, in a society whose values are precisely those of health, wealth and happiness. Look at the number of medical dramas and documentaries on television: is our obsession with the medical profession not a function of our obsession with health? Listen to the politicians: New Labour finance ministers say they want to reward 'risk takers'. Are they referring to the men and women who work in the slums with the drug addicts, who bravely stand against the paramilitary control of their communities in Ulster, who go to areas of conflict and put their lives on the line, who take 'real risks'? Of course not. They mean the entrepreneurs and the 'wealth creators' – often those whose sole motive (whatever the altruistic rhetoric) is personal profit and whose only 'risks' are the irresponsible financial speculations in which they indulge with the hard-earned savings and pensions of others. These are the counterfeit 'risk takers' that society must apparently prioritise and reward with tax breaks, gongs, and social status. If the real risk-takers need money, they can always queue up with their begging bowls outside the Ministry of Greed, aka the National Lottery, and take their turn with the rest of society's no-hopers and second-class causes. And look at the veritable explosion in the litigation and compensation arena: once upon a time, compensation was linked to loss of earnings; now it is often apparently linked to loss of comfort and happiness, with all of the trivial court cases that inevitably brings in its wake. Health, wealth, and happiness – the three modern obsessions, the three modern idols.

Where does the church stand in all this? Where do we as individual Christians put ourselves in relation to what is going on? One could write a huge tome on the subject but, within the limits of this editorial, I will confine my observations to just one or two 'litmus tests'.

First, let us look at the contemporary language of worship. Now, worship is a difficult subject and, being a peace-loving sort of chap who always steers well clear of controversy, I would hate to say anything controversial at this point about the relative merits of hymns and choruses, of organs and music bands etc. Having experienced – and generally appreciated – worship across the whole evangelical spectrum, from Charismatic to Reformed – I am myself less concerned here with the form of worship than I am with its content. Thus, I would like to make just one observation: the psalms, the Bible's own hymnbook, have almost entirely dropped from view in the contemporary Western evangelical scene. I am not certain about why this should be, but I have an instinctive feel that it has more than a little to do with the fact that a high proportion of the psalter is taken up with lamentation, with feeling sad, unhappy, tormented, and broken. In modern Western culture, these are simply not emotions which have much credibility: sure, people still feel these things, but to admit that they are a normal part of one's everyday life is tantamount to admitting that one has failed in today's health, wealth, and happiness society. And, of course, if one does admit to them, one must neither accept them nor take any personal responsibility for them: one must blame one's parents, sue one's employer, pop a pill, or check into a clinic in order to have such dysfunctional emotions soothed and one's self-image restored.

Now, one would not expect the world to have much time for the weakness of the psalmists' cries. It is very disturbing, however, when these cries of lamentation disappear from the language and worship of the church. Perhaps the Western church feels no need to lament – but then it is sadly deluded about how healthy it really is in terms of numbers, influence and spiritual maturity. Perhaps – and this is more likely – it has drunk so deeply at the well of modern Western materialism that it simply does not know what to do with such cries and regards them as little short of embarrassing. Yet the human condition is a poor one – and Christians who are aware of the deceitfulness of the human heart and are looking for a better country should know this. A diet of unremittingly jolly choruses and hymns inevitably creates an unrealistic horizon of expectation which sees the normative Christian life as one long triumphalist street party – a theologically incorrect and a pastorally disastrous scenario in a world of broken individuals. Has an unconscious belief that Christianity is – or at least should be – all about health, wealth, and happiness silently corrupted the content of our worship? Few Christians in areas where the church has been strongest over recent decades – China, Africa, Eastern Europe – would regard uninterrupted emotional highs as normal Christian experience. Indeed, the biblical portaits of believers give no room to such a notion. Look at Abraham, Joseph, David, Jeremiah, and the detailed account of the psalmists' experiences. Much agony, much lamentation, occasional despair – and joy, when it manifests itself – is very different from the frothy triumphalism that has infected so much of our modern Western Christianity. In the psalms, God has given the church a language which allows it to express even the deepest agonies of the human soul in the context of worship. Does our contemporary language of worship reflect the horizon of expectation regarding the believer's experience which the psalter proposes as normative? If not, why not? Is it because the comfortable values of Western middle-class consumerism have silently infiltrated the church and made us consider such cries irrelevant, embarrassing, and signs of abject failure?

I did once suggest at a church meeting that the psalms should take a higher priority in evangelical worship than they generally do – and was told in no uncertain terms by one indignant person that such a view betrayed a heart that had no interest in evangelism. On the contrary, I believe it is the exclusion of the experiences and expectations of the psalmists from our worship – and thus from our horizons of expectation – which has in a large part crippled the evangelistic efforts of the church in the West and turned us all into spiritual pixies. By excluding the cries of loneliness, dispossession, and desolation from its worship, the church has effectively silenced and excluded the voices of those who are themselves lonely, dispossessed, and desolate, both inside and outside the church. By so doing, it has implicitly endorsed the banal aspirations of consumerism, generated an insipid, trivial and unrealistically triumphalist Christianity, and confirmed its impeccable credentials as a club for the complacent. In the last year, I have asked three very different evangelical audiences what miserable Christians can sing in church. On each occasion my question has elicited uproarious laughter, as if the idea of a broken-hearted, lonely, or despairing Christian was so absurd as to be comical – and yet I posed the question in all seriousness. Is it any wonder that British evangelicalism, from the Reformed to the Charismatic, is almost entirely a comfortable, middle-class phenomenon?

One might also look at the content of prayers – those we speak in private and those at the church meeting. How often did Abraham, Moses, and Paul pray for health, for worldly success, for personal happiness and satisfaction? How do the concerns of these men compare with the content and priorities of our own prayers? Do our intercessions, despite the pious theological padding, unwittingly mimic the blasphemous priorities of the Elmer Gantrys of this world who peddle a pernicious gospel of health, wealth, and happiness?

Then, look at our own aspirations. I often chat to theological students and ask them what they intend to do on completion of their work. Many say they think they will enjoy teaching RE, some say that they are looking forward to doing research. Very few say, in the first instance, they want to serve the church. Now, one can serve the church in both of the aforementioned ways, but is it not significant that their first reaction is not to express themselves in terms of service but in terms of personal satisfaction? And the church as a whole is little better: big houses, flash cars, double incomes – all feature in the dreams of many of us, wrapped up as we are in making personal comfort and satisfaction our primary goal. Yet we should not build our lives on the basis of personal satisfaction but on the vision of self-sacrifice and service that the Bible lays before us. Given the choice, what would many of us involved in the professional theological sphere, students and academics, do: speak at a major academic gathering and hob-nob with the great and the good, or talk to the church youth group? Of course, many times we can do both – but what if we had to make a choice? The answer will speak eloquently of where our real treasure is stored. Has the gospel of our own personal ambition not upstaged the gospel of sacrificial service? It is faithfulness, not happiness or worldly reputation, which is the criterion of Christian success.

The church in the West is caught in a maelstrom of decline. One might suggest a whole variety of ways to overcome this. Some suggest we need to be more 'postmodern' in our worship; others suggest we need to rethink how the gospel is communicated. I confess to being sceptical about these proposals, not because they are too radical but because they are not radical enough. They reduce the causes for decline to the level of methodology or sociology and offer relatively painless remedies to what is, if we are honest, a very serious, even terminal, disease. Indeed, those who see the problem exclusively in these terms are merely replicating the kind of solutions which the very health, wealth, and happiness culture itself would propose: in the consumer culture, Christianity is a product, and poor sales

can therefore be overcome by new management, better packag-
ing and more astute marketing. Now I am not suggesting that
sociologists and postmodernists have nothing useful to tell us
– we must, of course, take care that we present the gospel in a
way in which society can understand it (though to describe that
as 'common sense' rather than 'postmodern', 'postevangelical'
or 'post-whatever' would seem on the whole to be less pretentious and obfuscatory) – but we must remember that to reduce
Western Christianity's difficulties to the level of bad technique
is to miss the point: the real problem is ultimately one of morality, not methodology. Quite simply, the evangelical church has
sold its soul to the values of Western society and prostituted
itself before the Golden Calf of materialism. Our current decline
is thus not in the final analysis simply the result of secularisation; it is ultimately the result of the active judgment of God
upon that secularisation. We have bought into the idolatry of
the secular values of health, wealth, and happiness, and until
we all, on both the individual and corporate level, realise this,
repent of it, and give ourselves in painful, sacrificial service to
the Lord who bought us, we will see no improvement.

How can we do this? First, let us all learn once again to lament. Read the psalms over and over until you have the vocabulary, grammar, and syntax necessary to lay your heart before God
in lamentation. If you do this, you will have the resources to cope
with your own times of suffering, despair and heartbreak, and
to keep worshipping and trusting through even the blackest of
days; you will also develop a greater understanding of fellow
Christians whose agonies of, say, bereavement, depression, or
despair, sometimes make it difficult for them to prance around
in ecstasy singing 'Jesus wants me for a sunbeam' on a Sunday
morning; and you will have more credible things to say to those
shattered and broken individuals – be they burned-out bank
managers or down-and-out junkies – to whom you may be called
to be a witness of God's unconditional mercy and grace to the
unloved and the unlovely. For such, as the Bible might put it,
were some of you...

Second, seek to make the priorities of the biblical prayers the priorities of your own prayers. You can read all the trendy sociology and postmodern primers you want, and they may well give you valuable technical insights, but unless your studies, your preaching, your church life, your family life, indeed, your whole life, are soaked in prayer and reflect the priorities of the Bible, they will be of no profit to you or to anybody else.

And finally, as regards personal ambitions and life-plans, 'Your attitude should be the same as Christ Jesus: Who, being in very nature God, did not consider equality with God something to be grasped, but made himself nothing, taking the very nature of a servant, being made in human likeness. And being found in appearance as a man, he humbled himself and became obedient to death – even death on a cross.'

THREE

THE MARCIONS HAVE LANDED!

When one asks who is one of the most influential thinkers in the modern evangelical church, one might think of names such as Jim Packer, John Stott, and Don Carson. I would like to suggest, however, that there is one whose influence is perhaps much greater than we are aware of, yet whose thinking all but pervades the modern evangelical church: Marcion. He's the man who gets my vote for most profound influence on evangelicalism, from canon to theology to worship practices. You never see his books on the shelves in your high street Christian bookshop; you never see him advertised as preaching in your local church; but, rest assured, his spirit stalks those bookshops and pulpits.

Marcion is – or, rather, was – a somewhat shadowy figure, with most of what we know about him coming from the hostile pen of Tertullian. Apparently, he was a native of Pontus (in modern times, the area by the Black Sea), who flourished in the middle of the second century, dying circa 160. His major distinctive was his insistence on the Christian gospel as exclusively one of love to the extent that he came to a complete rejection of the Old Testament and only a qualified acceptance of those parts of the New Testament which he considered to be consistent with his central thesis (i.e., ten letters of Paul and a recension of the Gospel of Luke).

So how does Marcion influence modern evangelicalism? Well, I think evangelicalism has become practically Marcionite at a number of levels.

First, the emphasis upon God's love to the utter exclusion of everything else has become something of a commonplace. We see this in the collapse of the notion of penal substitution as an evangelical doctrine. Now, maybe I'm missing something, but of all the things taught in the Bible, the terrifying wrath of God would seem to be among the most self-evident of all. Thus, when

I hear statements from evangelical theologians such as 'God's wrath is always restorative,' my mind goes straight to count-less Old Testament passages, the Bible's teaching about Satan, and New Testament characters such as Ananias and Sapphira. There was not much restoration for any of these folk – or are being swallowed alive by the earth, consumed by holy fire and being struck dead for cheating the church actually therapeutic techniques intended to restore the individuals concerned? And when leading evangelicals tell me that penal substitution is tantamount to cosmic child abuse (don't laugh – this is seri-ously argued by some leading evangelical theologians), I'm left wondering whether I should sit down and explain the doctrine to them, or whether I should merely tell them to go away and grow up. Do they really expect the church to take such claims as serious theological reflection?

Then, there is the constant tendency to neglect the Old Testament in particular in our theological reflections and our devotional lives, both of which need to take full account of the Old Testament. We need to read the Bible as a whole, to un-derstand each passage, each verse, within the theological and narrative structure of the canon as a whole. As evangelicals we can often err by focusing purely on the straight doctrinal teach-ing of the letters in the New Testament and the great passages in John's Gospel. A New Testament scholar and friend once said to me that he thought the average evangelical's life would be pretty much unaffected if the whole Bible, except for the Gos-pel of John and the Letter to the Romans, simply disappeared. Hyperbole maybe, but probably not by much. We need a solid *biblical* theology – not one which downgrades everything to the level of economy at the expense of ontology but one which takes full account of the central narrative of the Bible and seeks to do justice even to those bits of the Bible we don't like.

Then, in our church practice, we need to take the Old Testa-ment more seriously. It astounds me, given the over-whelming use of psalms as central to gathered worship in the first four centuries, the absolute importance given to psalmody for the first two centuries of the post-Reformation Reformed churches, and the fact that the Book of Psalms is the only hymn book which can claim to be universal in its acceptance by the whole of Christendom and utterly inspired in all of its statements – it astounds me, I say, that so few psalms are sung in our worship services today. Moreover, often nothing seems to earn the scorn and derision of others more than the suggestion that more psalms should be sung in worship. Indeed, the last few years have seen a number of writers strike out against exclusive psalmody. Given that life is too short to engage in pointless polemics, I am left wondering which parallel universe these guys come from, where the most pressing and dangerous worship issue is clearly that people sing *too much* of the Bible in their services. How terrifying a prospect that would be! Imagine: people actually singing songs that express the full range of human emotion in their worship using words of which God has explicitly said 'These are mine!' Back here on Planet Earth, however, there is generally precious little chance of overloading on sound theology in song in most evangelical churches as the Marcion invasion is pretty much total and unopposed in the sphere of worship. Yet I for one prefer Athanasius to Marcion as a patristic thinker and, in his letter to Marcellinus, he gives one of the most beautiful and moving arguments for psalms in worship ever penned (available at www.athanasius.com/psalms/aletterm.htm). It is a pity more have not taken his words to heart.

So what will be the long-term consequences of this Marcionite approach to the Bible? Ultimately, I think it will push 'the God who is there' back into the realm of the unknowable and make our god a mere projection of our own psychology and our worship simply into group therapy sessions where we all come together to pretend we are feeling great. God is the God of Abraham, Isaac and Jacob – take that identity away and what do we have left? As the Old Testament is the context for the New Testament, so the neglect of the Old Testament leaves the New as more or less meaningless. As our reading, our sermons, and our times of corporate worship neglect and, sometimes, simply

ignore the Old Testament, we can expect a general impoverish-
ment of church life and, finally, a total collapse of evangelical
Christendom. Indeed, there are mornings when I wake up and
think that it's already all over, and that the church in the West
survives more by sheer force of personality, by hype and by
marketing ploys than by any higher power. We need to grasp
once again who God is in his fullness; we need to grasp who we
are in relation to him; and we need teaching and worship which
gives full-orbed expression to these things – and this will only
come when we in the West grow up, ditch the designer gods we
build from our pick-'n-mix Bible where consumer, not Creator,
is king, and give the whole Bible its proper place in our lives,
thinking and worship. Think truncated thoughts about God and
you'll get a truncated God; read an expurgated Bible and you
get an expurgated theology; sing mindless, superficial rubbish
instead of deep, truly emotional praise and you will eventually
become what you sing.

FOUR

A REVOLUTIONARY BALANCING ACT OR: WHY OUR THEOLOGY NEEDS TO BE A LITTLE LESS BIBLICAL

Having spent my undergraduate days studying at the feet of a Marxist ancient historian who, to this day, remains one of the most brilliant and inspiring teachers I have ever had the privilege to know, I have ever since been somewhat interested in the notion of revolution. In Marxist philosophy, revolution takes place when the movement of capital has created such social tensions that the group 'in charge', so to speak, is displaced by those whom they have previously governed. Thus, the feudal lords are displaced by the bourgeoisie, the bourgeoisie by the proletariat – unless, of course, the society happens to be in the Far East (but that's another story, and another of those exceptions which, to the faithful at least, proves the rule).

My own interest in revolutions, however, is slightly different. As an intellectual historian committed to the study of ideas and their functions in historical context, and the role of self-understanding in the formation of cultures and movements, I am fascinated by the problem which all successful revolutionaries must ultimately face: the transition from rebels with outsider status to establishment with insider status. This is, of course, one of the themes of George Orwell's wonderful satire, *Animal Farm*. Here, the move from animal to human is so seamless that the protagonists are unaware it is happening until, in the last scene, no difference can be discerned between pig and human. But it afflicts all revolutions: when do the revolutionaries stop fighting the battles of the past? When do they come to realize that their agenda must change, that the pendulum must swing back in the opposite direction? When do the particular useful insights that they bring to bear upon particular situations become not simply insights but overwhelming and exclusive ideologies which prevent them from seeing wider realities and which fundamentally distort their perception of, and responses to, reality?

The question is particularly pressing with regard to theology and the church because the need for balance is absolutely crucial if the church is to witness to God's truth to the world, and a failure to speak the whole counsel of God is a critical weakness in our testimony as Christians. The problem is, of course, that the theological history of the church is a history of revolutions, generally driven by correct concerns, but all needing to be subject to the searching criticism of God's Word.

The issue which particularly concerns me at the moment is what I might call the crisis in systematic theology. I'm not, of course, talking here about the crisis in systematic theology in the university setting. With no coherent epistemological or ontological basis to hold itself together, the university discipline has long ago collapsed into an incoherent mish-mash of courses of the 'Theology and ....' variety, where you insert your own particular concern or interest, be it women, ecology, politics, vegetarianism, or Tom and Jerry cartoons. Hey, it's a postmodern world, cartoons are as worthy of time and energy as starving children, and the unifying factor in our disciplines, if there is one, must be found in our own little universes, not in the God of revelation.

No, I'm talking about the crisis in systematic theology in the churches. Now, it is, I think, true to say that fifty years ago or so in the UK there was a major problem when it came to preaching: if it happened at all, it was often little more than pious platitudes or, in very conservative circles, a lifeless reiteration of the tradition. One of the great revolutions in the church has been that this is no longer the case. Good preaching and teaching, while still not universal, is more common than it once was. We have the Lloyd-Joneses, the Stotts, the Packers, and the countless less famous yet no less competent church leaders to thank for that. More recently, we also have the biblical-theological/redemptive-historical movement from Moore College, disseminated by such groups as the Proclamation Trust which has, perhaps more than any other movement over recent years, served to transform how churches read and teach the Bible. One might say, in fact, that if Lloyd-Jones led the revolution which placed preaching back at the centre of British evangelicalism, the biblical theology movement has led the second revolution which has put careful attention to Christ-centred exegesis back at the centre of preaching.

Now, all this is good and to be welcomed, and all that I say in the rest of this editorial should be read in that light. My question, however, is: have the revolutionaries become the new establishment, and are we therefore missing out on issues of crucial importance through turning the valid insights of biblical-theological preaching into ideologies which exclude other, necessary emphases? I raise the question because it seems to me, as I mix with students in the USA and the UK, that many of them have a good grasp of biblical theology. They understand that the Bible contains a narrative, that this narrative culminates in Christ, and that this imposes certain demands upon the way they exegete any given passage. The problem today is not what it was ten, twenty, or fifty years ago when fanciful pietistic exegesis and non-exegetical doctrinalism might have vied for centre stage in the church (or so we are told); it is, rather, that the triumph of biblical theology has been so complete in some quarters that we now need to realize that this new establishment might itself be generating problems of its own.

Well, what's wrong with a biblical-theological approach, you ask? Nothing, in and of itself. But the way it pans out has, I would suggest, sometimes been less than helpful. First, there is the problem of mediocrity. It is one thing for a master of biblical theology to preach it week after week; quite another for a less talented follower so to do. We all know the old joke about the Christian fundamentalist who, when asked what was grey, furry, and lived in a tree, responded that 'It sure sounds like a squirrel, but I know the answer to every question is "Jesus".' One of the problems I have with a relentless diet of biblical-theological sermons from less talented (i.e., most of us) preachers is their boring mediocrity: contrived contortions of passages which are engaged in to produce the answer 'Jesus' every week. It doesn't matter what the text is; the sermon is always the same.

Second, the triumph of the biblical-theological method in theology and preaching has come at the very high price of a neglect of the theological tradition. The church spent nearly seventeen hundred years engaging in careful doctrinal reflection; formulating a technical language allowing her theologians to express themselves with precision and clarity; writing creeds and confessions to allow believers over the face of the earth to express themselves with one voice; and wrestling long and hard with those aspects of God which must be true if the biblical record was to be at all coherent or make any sense whatsoever. Classic systematic theology was taught systematically, not because it was divorced from exegesis (no scholar of the Middle Ages or of the sixteenth and seventeenth centuries would argue such a ridiculous thing, although the claim is frequently heard in popular circles), but because the church had a firm understanding of the need for clear teaching, a confidence in the substantial unity of God's revelation, and a deep appreciation of the need to push beyond economic questions if there was to be such a thing as orthodoxy and it was to be defended in a coherent fashion. The economics of the history of salvation, on which the biblical theology movement is so good, was always carefully balanced by judicious reflection upon the ontological aspects of God which undergirded the whole of the church's life and history.

My greatest concern with the biblical theology movement is that it places such an overwhelming emphasis upon the economy of salvation that it neglects these ontological aspects of theology. In doing so, it will, I believe, prove ultimately self-defeating: a divine economy without a divine ontology is unstable and will collapse. Trinitarianism will dissolve into modalism; the theological unity of the Bible will be swallowed up and destroyed by its diversity because it has no foundation in the one God who speaks; and Christian exclusivism will be sacrificed to a mean-ingless pluralism as the church's narrative is reduced to having significance only within the bounds of the Christian community. I suspect that 'openness theism' is merely the most well-known heresy to have been nurtured in the anti-doctrine, anti-tradition world of contemporary evangelicalism; it will certainly not be the last. And my fear is that the overwhelming economic empha-sis of the biblical theology trajectory effectively cuts the church off from probing the ontological questions which I believe are demanded by reflection upon the biblical text, by consideration of the church's tradition, and by our Christian commitment to the notion of the existence of a God who has revealed himself yet whose existence is prior to that revelation.

The strategic problem, of course, is getting anyone to believe that this is so, and not just another one of Trueman's eccentric and pessimistic takes on contemporary evangelicalism. And that problem is really a function of the fact that the old bibli-cal-theological rebels have become the new establishment but have not yet realized this and have therefore not relativised their contribution accordingly. Important insights have become controlling ideologies which cut the church off from her tradi-tion and render her thereby impoverished. Biblical theology is – or rather, was – a necessary corrective to fanciful pietistic exegesis and mindless doctrinalism – but anyone who thinks that these are still the major problems in evangelical churches clearly inhabits a different world to the one of which I have experience. In most churches where preaching still holds a central place, I suspect that an overemphasis on doctrine and systematic theology is not the problem. After all, how many of us go to churches where the Trinitarian nature of God, while upheld in our doctrinal statements, is sidelined in preaching and worship to the point where most of us are functional Unitarians. In my experience as a teacher, it is a lack of knowledge of, say, the doctrine of the Trinity rather than puzzlement over how to preach a Christian sermon on David and Goliath which is today the most pressing problem.

Year in, year out, I teach the history of Christian doctrine; and, year in, year out, I have not only taken flack from those liberals for whom the whole idea of doctrine is somewhat fanciful; I have also taken flack from those evangelicals who 'just have their Bible'. That the church wrestled for at least 1700 years with issues of systematic theology, not just biblical narrative, and did so in a manner which sought to preserve the balance between economy and ontology in the church's proclamation of God in Christ, is lost on such students. My fear is that the biblical theology movement, while striving to place the Word back at the centre of the church's life, is inadequate in and by itself for the theological task of defending and articulating the faith. Reflection upon the wider church tradition is needed, creeds, confessions and all, because this is the best way to understand how and where the discipline of biblical theology and redemptive history can be of use to the wider picture without it usurping and excluding other, equally necessary and important theological disciplines. Christianity is Trinitarian at its very core, and it is my suspicion that biblical theology on its own is inadequate to protect and defend that core. We need ontology as well as economy if we are to do justice to the Bible's teaching on who God is and what he has done. The biblical-theological revolutionaries have become the new establishment; and it's time for those of us rebels who think that the Bible raises more than just redemptive-historical questions, and that the creedal tradition of the church gives important insights on this, to raise our voices in dissent, to highlight the very real dangers of making this insight into an ideology and to do our best to bring the pendulum back a little.

FIVE

BORING OURSELVES TO LIFE

As I write, Philadelphia is enduring the worst snowstorm since 1996, with upwards of twenty inches of snow predicted to fall within the next twenty-four hours. While I hate having to spend time clearing the pavement outside my house I must say that I am absolutely delighted that the storm has given me the unexpected pleasure of having a day off work to take my family sledging.

Yet the storm has been instructive to me in more than just the area of my winter sport skills. One of the most amusing sights on the television in recent days has been that of the queues of people in the shops stocking up on winter essentials in case they are trapped in their homes for any length of time. Now, by 'essentials,' I do not mean food, milk and other necessities. Hey, this is America after all; gargantuan consumption is virtually compulsory; and the average American refrigerator routinely carries enough supplies to feed the whole of Africa for a month, or the typical Western family for at least a week. No, I'm referring to American essentials, and the queues I am speaking of are the lines of people at the local video stores who, the TV reporter informs me, are stocking up on movies lest they get trapped in their homes and become bored.

My initial response to this gem of information was to burst out laughing. Perish the thought that any of these people should be so deprived of prepackaged entertainment that they might have to read a book, or (horror of horrors!) actually talk to other members of their families. Yet, on serious reflection, I realize the phenomenon is a very telling one, underlining once again that we in the West have become a decidedly entertainment-based culture. With no problems regarding supplies of essentials, the greatest fear that we have at any time of potential crisis is that we might be deprived of being amused for a whole forty-eight hours.

The entertainment world is a dominant factor in our consumer society. As both Marxists, and detectives in American
pulp fiction, well know, if you want to understand any given
situation, you should follow the money; thus, if you want to find
out what is important in any given society, you should simply
look to see where the money is – and there is surely no doubt
where the cash is to be found in the West of today: pop stars,
movie actors, sports figures – these are the people who earn the
real money in our world. Love him or hate him, the President
of the USA does basically shoulder responsibility for the safety
and stability of the world as a whole – but he earns peanuts
compared to even a modestly talented footballer or film star; and
the British public regularly expresses outrage at the exorbitant
pay rises of industry chiefs (an outrage I share, by the way) while
winking at the whopping salaries paid to teenage sports and pop
stars – salaries which help price event tickets out of the reach of
the ordinary citizen – and the sickening photo-shoot fees paid
to some sleazy celebrity getting married for the umpteenth time.
It is a strange world where we begrudge the Prime Minister a
six-figure salary while continuing to patronize magazines which
pay himbos and bimbos hundreds of thousands of pounds for
meaningless trash.

Why do we do it? Probably there are numerous reasons, but
a prime factor has to be the useful role which we see celebrities
playing in our society. They entertain us, and that, we think, is
a good thing, worth paying for – indeed worth paying more for
than good government and better public services. And why do
we think this way? Well, one interpretation offered by some
is that there is, in fact, a spiritual dimension to this culture of
celebrity and entertainment. Sports figures, pop stars, celebrities – they offer us meaning and fulfilment, albeit vicariously, in
a world where the old gods of traditional religions have failed.
Thus, at its apex, this culture produces new messianic figures,
such as Elvis or John Lennon, and icons, such as James Dean,
David Beckham, and Princess Diana. The deification of these
figures in modern culture, it is argued, indicates that there is

something innate in human beings that strives for transcendence, for something beyond the routine of everyday life.

Well, that is one take on the phenomenon, and one that enjoys considerable currency in some evangelical quarters. There is, however, another way of approaching this matter, a way which receives its clearest articulation in the thought of the great French thinker, Blaise Pascal. Pascal lived in a world which was marked both by its incredible busy-ness and by its appetite, at least among the social elite, for pleasure and entertainment. Pascal categorized this phenomenon as *distraction*. Distraction is the production of entertainment for the purpose of taking one's mind off the deeper realities of life. In a famous paragraph in the *Pensées*, he asks why even kings have trivial entertainments organized for their amusement. He can understand, he says, why poor people might enjoy the odd dance to distract them from the miserable drudge of their daily lives, but why should a king, glorious, powerful, surrounded by proofs of his own greatness, need trivial entertainment? The answer is that, left to himself with nothing to distract him, he will think about himself and the reality of the death that awaits him.[1]

Surely this is precisely what is going on in the contemporary culture of entertainment and celebrity. Why do we pay sports stars, actors, and the various airheads that populate the airwaves more than we pay our political leaders? Because they help to take our minds off the deeper, more demanding truths of life, particularly the one great and ultimately unavoidable truth: death. And it's not just the entertainment industry that does that: the huge amount of money expended on the health industry in general and the cosmetic surgery industry in particular also point us towards the basic drive in society to avoid this one at all costs. As Pascal himself says, 'It is easier to put up with death without thinking about it, than with the idea of death when there is no danger of it.'[2]

---

1. Blaise Pascal, *Pensées*, trans. Honor Levi (Oxford: World's Classics, 1995), 48-49.
2. *Pensées*, 49.

Pascal goes further, arguing that not just entertainment, or distraction, subserves this greater end of self-deception; even the social and bureaucratic clutter of our everyday commerce in this world has a similar significance. This he describes not as distraction but as 'diversion'. Let me quote him at length on this:

> From childhood onwards people are entrusted with the care of their honour, their property, their friends, and even with the property of their friends. They are showered with duties, the need to learn languages and exercises. They are led to believe that they will never be happy if their health, honour, and wealth, and those of their friends, are not in a satisfactory state, and that if one element is amiss they will be unhappy. So they are given offices and duties which keep them hectically occupied from daybreak.[3]

This ties in with distraction in that the two work together to fill the lives of men and women with ephemeral trivia so that whatever time is left after such diversions is to be devoted to entertainment and pleasure. To express the idea in modern form: once you have spent most of your day dealing with the nightmare that is the modern workplace, you get home and switch on your TV or go to the movies, being entertained or projecting some fantasy on to a celebrity figure. Then when you fear being trapped in your house by snow, for example, your first concern is to make sure that the supply of prepackaged entertainment does not dry up, lest the boredom of your enforced isolation force you to think about your mortal condition. Only in this way can you avoid facing up to your own mortality. Pascal ends the passage with a phrase which, literally translated, says 'How hollow and full of excrement is the heart of man,' meaning 'How we fill our lives with rubbish instead of reflecting upon real truths.' We would rather spend time and money on junk than spend a single moment thinking about where our lives are really heading.

Pascal is not, of course, saying that entertainment is wrong in and of itself, any more than hard work or concern for the well-

3. *Pensées*, p. 49.

being of one's family is illegitimate. Though he himself lived a fairly rigorous ascetic life, his point is not to outlaw all pleasure but rather to criticize the use of entertainment as a way of distracting men and women from the realities of life. Pleasure and fun are good things; but when they become means of keeping us from facing up to the truths of our creaturely existence, they are profoundly bad for us.

This approach puts a very different complexion, of course, on the modern world. The obsession with sex, with drugs, with celebrity worship, with weird and wonderful cults, and even with conspicuous consumption and shopping– these are not signs of some deep quest for spiritual meaning, of attempts to fill some religious void in lives that we somehow know are incomplete in and of themselves; rather than being hopeful signs of humanity's innate spirituality, they are in fact the latest attempts of humanity to avoid precisely any form of true spirituality. They represent not ill-informed striving after truth and meaning but pathetic efforts to pretend that we are not going to die and then to face the judgment; they are, in short, acts which seek to suppress the truth in unrighteousness and to avoid the claims of Christ, in whom is revealed the full reality both of God's judgment and his grace.

This is where boredom is so important. Stripped of diversions and distractions, individuals have no choice but to reflect upon themselves, the reality of their lives and their future deaths. Human culture has proved adept over the centuries at avoiding the claims of Christ and the truths of human existence revealed in him; and the modern bureaucratic state, the instability and insecurity of the work environment, the entertainment industry and the consumer society in which our modern Western affluence allows us to indulge, all play their part in keeping us from reflecting upon reality as revealed to us by God. Let us take time, then, to be bored, to strip away from ourselves the screens we have created to hide the real truths of life and death from our eyes. Let us spend less time trying to appropriate culture for Christianity and more time deconstructing culture in the light of Christ's claims on us and the world around us. Only then, I think, will we truly grasp the urgency of the human predicament. And if it snows again, don't rent a video; read a copy of Pascal's *Pensées*.

SIX

WHY YOU SHOULDN'T BUY THE BIG ISSUE

By the time this edition of *Themelios* comes out, the noise and drama of the debate over homosexuality in the Anglican church will probably have died down somewhat – though we can be certain this will only be a temporary lull. The issue is not set to disappear any time soon; and the passions which run deep on both sides of the debate are unlikely to abate over time. Indeed, for many in the church, it is without doubt the Big Issue of our time.

The whole thing is, of course, a gift to the media. A Christian denomination openly divided against itself; endless TV appearances of awkward-looking men in ridiculously outdated outfits that make your elderly grandparents look like cutting-edge fashionistas; and the interminable waffle and meaningless jargon which seem to serve no purpose other than to cloud the basic points at issue – all of this helps the men and women who bring us the news to portray the church as irrelevant to the world of the present day, little more than a tragicomic turn for the 'And finally....' section of the nightly news. And if Anglicanism has taken a beating, other mainline British denominations have also been thrashed, their unfortunate leaders looking hopelessly out of their depth when confronted with a ruthless and savvy media.

In this climate, there is one question which needs to be asked, and that not of the media or the liberals within these churches – both of these groups are, at bottom, fairly easy to understand. The newspaper owners, the TV moguls, and all of their underlings are in the business of good copy. If it sells, then it's worth reporting; and sex, particularly when you make it gay sex and throw in religion for good measure, sells more than most. As for liberal theologians – well, they've long played the game of baptizing and sanctifying today the moral and sexual standards of the world of yesterday, thereby dooming themselves to being always at least twenty-four hours out-of-date.

No, the question to ask is: why is it that disagreement over the issue of the Bible's teaching on homosexuality has become the apparent bridge too far for the evangelicals in mainline denominations, the issue on which they are prepared to make such a stand? Now, don't get me wrong – I certainly regard the legitimisation of homosexual relationships by any church or denomination as flying in the face of clear scriptural teaching; but, let's face it, sexual morality is not the only, or even the central, thing which scripture teaches; and we have had in the past Anglican bishops who deny the deity of Christ, his substitutionary atonement, his resurrection, and the final and unique authority of his scriptures, to name but four of the most basic points of kindergarten Christian orthodoxy. Yet few if any in the mainlines seem to have regarded these as put-up-or-shut-up issues.

Given the long-standing existence within mainline churches of all manner of heresy, I have to confess to being as confused as many in the Gay movement over the evangelical histrionics surrounding the issue of the Bible's teaching on homosexuality: if all manner of blasphemy is acceptable in the church, why make homosexuality *the* issue to fight over? Indeed, these days I find myself in the strange situation of having to agree with many of the gay critics of the stance of evangelicals in mainline denominations: the unique status evangelicals seem to have decided to accord to homosexuality makes it look to the wider world as if their motives are not those of consistent care for Christian orthodoxy but homophobia, pure and simple. Apparently, we can live with bishops who argue the case against Christ; but we must not tolerate those who argue the case for homosexuality. Now, I know personally many of those involved in the fight, and I know that they are not homophobic; but imagine how the current situation appears to the uninitiated, to the outsiders who do not know the internal workings of the British evangelical world – it looks suspiciously like basic prejudice against gay people rather than serious concern for Christian orthodoxy.

How things have reached such a state of confusion and hysteria is a complex and convoluted story; but it is hard not to
conclude that the situation has highlighted serious weaknesses
within the popular front evangelicalism of the mainline denominations which have led, inadvertently no doubt, to a hopelessly
confused and inconsistent Christian witness on central doctrinal issues, such as the resurrection, and on important ethical
issues, such as homosexuality.

First, if we are honest, there is a tendency within all of us to
have an attitude towards orthodoxy which is something akin
to 'given the truth, what can I get away with? How can I twist
things to allow me to get out from under some of the personally
more inhibiting or culturally more embarrassing aspects of the
Christian faith?' For decades, we evangelicals have been spinning
like tops on issues such as the authority of scripture, the death
of Christ, the nature of church leadership etc. in ways that allow
for enough acknowledgement of the traditional vocabulary on
these issues to keep constituencies, power-bases and evangelical
paymasters happy, but which really open up the potential for
significant deviation from the orthodox trajectories of the use
and intent of such language, particularly when we want to seem
scholarly / tolerant / enlightened / hip or whatever to the wider
world. The sad thing is that, when vocabulary developed by the
church over many years to make precise and clear statements
about certain matters subsequently comes to take on very vague
and often indeterminate meanings, the scene is set for linguistic
and theological anarchy. We can no longer resist heterodoxy
and heresy, or determine which issues are primary and which
secondary, because we have destroyed the very conceptual vocabulary which we could have used for just such a purpose. One
might also add at this point that the hermeneutical overload in
some branches of contemporary evangelicalism has, ironically,
not simply injected a little appropriate cultural and historical
modesty into our theological endeavours but also frequently
served only to make the Bible a more obscure, vague and complicated book than ever, with the insidious 'Did God really say...'

being perhaps a more accurate summary of the teaching heard in some evangelical quarters than the prophetic 'Thus says the LORD...' We have sown the linguistic wind; and we are just now feeling the first cold blasts of the heretical whirlwind.

Second, the lack of a proper reflection upon the church in evangelical circles has had a series of most unfortunate consequences. Those who see the Christian life in individual terms, who see themselves, or their individual congregation, as the centre of the theological universe, are doomed to make their personal issues, or those of their particular congregation, the most important problems facing Christianity. We see this most clearly perhaps in the modern aversion to signing creeds or doctrinal statements. We often say this is because we have no creed but the Bible; but in practice it is often because we do not want to submit ourselves to any form of public authority or scrutiny, preferring our own individual, frequently ill-informed, and not uncommonly idiosyncratic interpretations of scripture. The result is too often a pick-n-mix Christianity where each believes what is right in his or her own eyes. If we took more seriously the great creeds and confessions of the church over the centuries, we would at least have some insight into what the church has over millennia considered to be important and necessary to a correct understanding of the Bible.

Third, the battle cry of 'Exegesis, exegesis, exegesis!' that I hear coming from some sections of the evangelical world has its shortcomings here as well. Of course, exegesis is a basic element of all sound theology; but, like the foundations or frame of a house, if that's all there is, you're going to get wet, very wet, when it rains. It can lead to a fragmentary approach to the Bible which never sees the whole picture, or the priorities which exist within the overall witness of scripture. It can be profoundly anti-intellectual, eschewing all questions that a superficial reading of the text does not raise. Its frequent failure to rise to theological and ethical synthesis, and to engage modestly and thoughtfully with the priorities of the creedal and confessional trajectories of the church, leaves it inadequate to deal with really big issues in any kind of historical, social or ecclesiastical perspective. Exegesis is important; but it needs to stand in relation to other theological and ethical tasks if it is not to prove itself the basis for a highly unstable, selective and inconsistent church policy. Preachers, as well as believers, have their pick-'n-mix priorities, against which the testimony of the centuries, embodied in the creeds and confessions, can go some way to help. No-one, therefore, should be allowed within a million miles of a pulpit who does not have a proper respect for biblical theology in terms of the overall story of redemptive history, a firm grasp of the importance of systematic theology, creeds and confessions, and a critical handle on contemporary culture. Only then can he begin to deal with the latest big thing in any kind of biblical, theological and historical perspective.

Let me make myself clear at this point: I consider any move by churches to recognize as legitimate the sexual union of homosexual and lesbian partners to be at fundamental odds with the clear teaching of scripture. It is an offence to God's holiness and, moreover, it is pastorally cruel and callous to the highest degree, effectively denying those involved the possibility of repentance for sin and of God's love and grace. I also consider the holding of office in a church by someone who is openly committed to living in a homosexual relationship to be a travesty of Paul's teaching about the qualities necessary for those called to lead in the congregation of the saints. But, then again, I also consider denial of the resurrection, the trashing of scriptural authority, the mocking of the death of Christ, and the casual trampling of any number of cardinal theological truths also to be at odds with scripture and to be just as pastorally cruel and callous. For me, homosexuality is not *the* issue; it is rather a symptom of our failure in these other areas; and to treat this as some kind of Rubicon is to misread the signs of the times. Check Romans 1: homosexuality is not a *provocation* of God's judgment so much as a *sign* of God's judgment. Do not think that we evangelicals in the northern hemisphere are going down the theological pan because of homosexuality; the problems we face with homosexuality indicate that the process of collapse and decline has been underway for many years. I for one cannot therefore expend huge emotional energy on this particular symptom; I think rather that we need to go deeper and address the foundational issues which have brought us to this sorry pass. The only big issue in this age, as in any age, is the reality of Jesus Christ; and churches in Britain and the USA have allowed men and women who deny this reality to occupy pulpits for decades; are our evangelical leaders then really surprised that, having allowed such supreme pastoral cruelty to exist for so long, all other areas of biblical teaching are gradually being dispatched to the theological landfill site?

And for those who disagree and think that disagreement over the Bible's teaching on homosexuality is the big one, the church's do-or-die moment – well, you are free to do so; but do spend some time reflecting on how, when gay friends ask you why homosexuality is *the* big issue, you are going to answer them in a way which at least looks consistent with historic Christianity and does not simply appear to be the result of some irrational homophobia. My advice: don't buy the big issue as either the world or much of the current evangelical leadership in the mainlines tries to sell it to you; think biblically, with Christ at the centre.

POSTSCRIPT

EVANGELICALISM THROUGH THE LOOKING GLASS: A FAIRY TALE

As Alice was walking down the road, she saw, sitting high up on a fence, a strange looking creature rather like an egg.

'How curious you look,' she called up to the man. 'What kind of person are you?'

'My name,' said the egg, 'is Humpty Dumpty. And what, pray, is yours?'

'Alice,' said Alice. 'And why do you sit so high up on that fence?'

'My task is the protection of the truth of evangelicalism through the preservation of fellowship and peace between the people who live on either side of this fence.'

'That is very interesting,' said Alice. 'Tell me, what exactly do you mean by evangelicalism?'

'I mean all those from whatever country who agree on the basics of Christianity, that God is sovereign, humanity fell in Adam, justification is by grace through faith via the imputation of Christ's righteousness. Stuff like that.' Humpty sniffed and looked up to the sky. 'Such childish questioning!' he muttered to himself.

'Curiouser and curiouser,' said Alice. 'I have never heard of these things. Perhaps you would like to explain them to me?'

'Hmm,' grumbled Humpty, not used to being subjected to such shameless interrogation. 'I am most exceedingly busy, little girl, but, as you are so ignorant, I shall try to lighten your darkness. To say that God is sovereign is to say that God is in complete control of all that goes on, that he knows the past, the present and the future. It is also, I am glad to say, a definition broad enough to include the claim that God is not in complete control of things and that, while he knows the past and the present, he has some severe blind spots when it comes to the

187

future. As for the Fall, it means that when Adam disobeyed God in the Garden, the whole status of humanity was changed, that he was driven from the Garden and that all those descended from him are subject always to avoiding God's presence at every opportunity. Upon this, we are all, I am pleased to announce, completely agreed – except, of course, for those who think that Adam never existed and that humanity is essentially sound. Still, the basics of the position are held in common by dwellers on both sides of this fence. As for justification by imputation, it means that we stand before God clothed only in the righteousness of Christ and that it is only as we trust God that we are given this status of righteousness. There is absolute unanimity on that – except, of course that no intelligent reader of the Bible on the far side of the fence really believes it any more. Nevertheless, this does not undermine our unity on the issue.'

Alice, somewhat perplexed, looked at the strange egg-shaped man. 'But is it not nonsense to say that those in such fundamental disagreement can agree to a formula of words? Does it not require that words can mean one thing and also their complete opposite?'

'My, my, you are a naive child, aren't you?' said Humpty. 'Has nobody ever told you that meaning is only in the mind of the reader, not the text?'

'I confess, sir,' said Alice, 'that I have heard such arguments but have always felt that, in the realm of Christianity, holding as it does to the idea of the God who has spoken, and of a loving heavenly Father who is of a kind that will not give his children a stone if they ask for bread, such a two-faced position was less than biblical. And indeed, is it not the case that for anyone, especially a Christian, to affirm public belief in something in which they don't actually believe, is an act lacking in personal integrity? What you propose indicates that there is a moral void at the heart of your position.'

'You forget,' laughed Humpty, 'that one man's personal integrity is another man's narrow-minded fundamentalism! And what you so offensively call "a moral void", I call "biblical Christian breadth" or, better still, "a sound attempt to revision Christian theology for the postmodern world of Generation X." You really must not be so bigoted, you know! The important thing is to *act* like a Christian. Now, please, take your self-righteous fundamentalist extremism elsewhere.'

Alice, deeply upset by the last jibe, shouted up at the egg: 'Sir, you play games with me. Does acting like a Christian not involve first and foremost being honest about what one believes, about not saying one thing and doing another in order to gain a platform, audience or credibility? You are not using these words with their proper meaning.'

'When I use a word,' Humpty Dumpty said in rather a scornful tone, 'it means just what I choose it to mean – neither more nor less.'

'The question is,' said Alice, 'whether you *can* make words mean different things.'

'The question is,' said Humpty Dumpty, 'which is to be master – that's all.'

'And who *is* master?' cried Alice. 'To whom are you accountable?'

Humpty Dumpty leaned down as far as he could without losing his seat on the fence and patted Alice on the head. 'My dear, dear, young girl, rest assured that I am master and certainly not the words themselves. And I and my friends are accountable to no-one – and certainly not to such a naive and impudent young thing as yourself.'

'Be careful, Humpty,' Alice warned. 'That fence is exceedingly narrow and you might well find yourself falling off it if you insist on trying to do justice to those of us on both sides.'

'Nonsense!' cried Humpty. 'Whatever you mean by "narrow", I see it as exceedingly wide with plenty of room for all.' Then, leaning closer, he hissed in her ear, 'But, if I do happen to fall, have no fear – I have no intention of coming down on your side of the fence. Your view of words is so exceedingly narrow and your view of integrity so antiquated, so bibliolatrous, so – so – *rationalist*, that I fear I should never find a fence to sit upon in your land.'

Alice felt a shiver go down her spine. 'On that,' she said, 'we can both agree.'

Alice waited a minute to see if he would speak again, if he wished her to stay, if he would come to a realisation of the basic incoherence of his position but, as he never opened his eyes or took any further notice of her, she said 'Good-bye!' and, on getting no answer to this, she quietly walked away; but she couldn't help saying to herself as she went, 'Of all the unsatisfactory people I ever met....' She never finished the sentence, for at this moment a heavy crash shook the forest from end to end.

Evangelical Concerns

Rediscovering the Christian mind on issues facing the Church today

Melvin Tinker

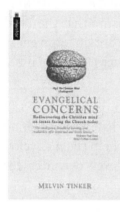

When we survey the world around us we can be left with the eerie feeling that evangelicals stand in the shadows of a collapsing culture with two alternatives open to us: either to retreat into a ghetto or sell out on fundamental issues of truth. Here, Melvin Tinker suggests a 'Third Way' – to fully engage with the world whilst being firmly rooted in the Word. In other words developing a fully-orbed biblical approach to science and socio-political issues – and so to regain the Christian mind.

'These Essays show an acute perception of the way that evangelicalism is going, and of the ways of returning it to the 'old paths'. Their intelligence, breadth of learning, and readability offer important and timely lessons for evangelicals of all hues.'

Paul Helm, Emeritus Professor, University of London

'Christians need to think deeply, and biblically about the issues facing society today. Melvin Tinker offers us a refreshing and insightful way into many such issues.'

David Cook, BBC Radio 4's "The Moral Maze"

'...Melvin Tinker's bold, prophetic witness comes at what may turn out to be a key turning point for the future of the church.'

Gerald Bray, Beeson Divinity School, Birmingham, Alabama

Melvin Tinker is Minister of St John's Parish Church in Newlands, Hull, England.

ISBN 978-1-85792-675-0

Christian Focus Publications

publishes books for all ages,
Our mission statement –

STAYING FAITHFUL

In dependence upon God we seek to help make His infallible Word, the Bible, relevant. Our aim is to ensure that the Lord Jesus Christ is presented as the only hope to obtain forgiveness of sin, live a useful life and look forward to heaven with Him.

REACHING OUT

Christ's last command requires us to reach out to our world with His gospel. We seek to help fulfill that by publishing books that point people towards Jesus and help them develop a Christ-like maturity. We aim to equip all levels of readers for life, work, ministry and mission.

Books in our adult range are published in three imprints.

Christian Focus contains popular works including biographies, commentaries, basic doctrine and Christian living. Our children's books are also published in this imprint.

Mentor focuses on books written at a level suitable for Bible College and seminary students, pastors, and other serious readers. The imprint includes commentaries, doctrinal studies, examination of current issues and church history.

Christian Heritage contains classic writings from the past.

Christian Focus Publications, Ltd
Geanies House, Fearn,
Ross-shire, IV20 1TW,
Scotland, United Kingdom
info@christianfocus.com

For details of our titles visit us on our website
www.christianfocus.com